The C-47

Flying Workhorse of WW II

By

Richard D. Harvey

authorHOUSE™

1663 LIBERTY DRIVE, SUITE 200
BLOOMINGTON, INDIANA 47403
(800) 839-8640
WWW.AUTHORHOUSE.COM

First published by AuthorHouse 03/10/05

ISBN: 1-4208-1699-3 (e)
ISBN: 1-4208-1698-5 (sc)

Printed in the United States of America
Bloomington, Indiana

This book is printed on acid-free paper.

Thank you to Norm Taylor for providing the photograph of the C-47 airplane on the front cover of this book. Both the inside photo and back cover photo of Lt. Richard Harvey are property of the author. Cover Design and Editing by Shannon Rogers.

"There are a thousand thoughts lying within a man that he does not know till he takes up a pen to write." - William Makepeace Thackeray

This book is dedicated to "THE 60ᵗʰ TROOP CARRIER GROUP" in particular and to every man or woman who ever put on a uniform and did his or her bit to guarantee our continued FREEDOM here in America.

I give my heartfelt thanks to my granddaughter, Shannon Rogers, for her knowledge of and the ability to use the computer. She gave much of her time in designing the book - - and putting my manuscript on the proper discs for the publisher. Without her help, this book would have died in the File 13! Thank you! Thank you Shannon!

FOREWORD

World War II was the single greatest and most far-reaching event of the 20th century. The sacrifices the United States made were staggering. More than 16 million of our best and brightest were in uniform. More than 400,000 made the supreme sacrifice, almost 700,000 were wounded, while 78,000 remain missing. Fewer than 4 million veterans from that conflict are still living, with 1,250 leaving this world of sight and sound every day.

The United States spent an estimated $288 billion on World War II; the U.S. increased productivity 800% between 1941 and 1946 to produce military planes every 5 minutes and a new warship every day in order to assure final victory. To keep such an effort going, we had a nation that was united with every citizen doing his or her part to bring about that final victory.

Lt. Richard D. Harvey has written his story about those years between 1941 and 1946. It is a good read because it comes from the heart of a man who saw it all during those years of world conflict.

Lt. Harvey served, for most of the war, in the 60th Troop Carrier Group. His plane was the famous C-47 – "The Flying Workhorse of World War II" and was the most versatile plane ever built. As a paratrooper with the 2nd Marine Parachute Battalion, USMC, I can attest to this for it was from this plane that we jumped. How grateful we were for the skill and dedication of those pilots, like Lt. Harvey, who flew us safely to our destination.

General P.X. Kelley, USMC, at the dedication of the World War II Memorial in Washington, D.C. had it right when he said, "that our nation has sent its most precious treasures, its sons and daughters, to human conflicts beyond our shores – not to seize, not to subjugate, not to occupy but to preserve the inalienable right of all mankind to life, liberty and the pursuit of happiness".

This book will help us all to remember the sacrifices made by the World War II generation.

- R. Byron Crozier, U.S.N.

INTRODUCTION

In the early hours one snowy Indiana morning in February, I hunched over my typewriter and thought out loud, "This may be the first sentence of a totally disastrous endeavor". If it is, so be it. Nothing ventured, nothing gained!

I have been asked a number of times why I haven't written anything about my World War II experience. Truthfully, I have given it a great deal of thought, but until I read Stephen E. Ambrose's book *The Wild Blue*, I had dispelled the thought from my mind. I have read a number of books about various war experiences but *The Wild Blue* really got me thinking. Many, many interesting stories have been written about the war and about the Air Force, of which I was a part. In spite of this, I have yet to find anything in writing about the Troop Carrier Pilots and Crews and their exact roles in the war. Having been a Troop Carrier Pilot, I do have a little first hand knowledge of what they did when they were not preparing for an important Air-borne Troop drop. I have read a number of books about the Fighter Wings and Bomber Groups - all great pieces of work. My heart goes out to every one of them and the hell that they had to go through. This book is about the 60th Troop Carrier Group; it's conception and, our duties and responsibilities during and after the war in Europe.

After a great deal of thought and many sleepless nights, the title that seemed to fit this book best was *The C-47 – FLYING WORKHORSE OF WW II.* I dedicate this book to all the guys in the 60th Troop Carrier Group and particularly those in the 12th Squadron of which I was a part. I would like to say right up front that I have nothing but respect for everyone who served in the Air Force from the guys who flew in the Bomb Groups, the Fighter Groups, the Troop Carrier Groups and all the ground personnel who kept us in the air. I am sure there were many others assigned to the Air Force that I have not mentioned but these were the ones that we saw every day in one place or another. Every service man or woman gave his or her all in any capacity to help win the war. As much respect as I have for every person in the service, be they Air Force, Army, Navy, Marines, Coast Guard or Merchant Marine my hat is off to them. My heart goes out especially to all those men on the ground in the trenches.

As I said before, every man or woman gave his or her all— but those serving on the ground suffered in much worse circumstances. When we returned during the day from a mission or a flight we had a bed to sleep in and decent food (most of the time!) Only once or twice do I remember having to sleep in the airplane on some far off field. For what it may mean I learned too, that the rank I came to respect the most were the Master Sergeants. I always felt that they earned every promotion that they ever got!

I think as you read you'll discover what all the C-47 did in just our group alone, multiply that by the other Troop Carrier Groups such as The Air Transport Groups (and Lord only knows where they were called upon) I think then you will realize why the title THE C-47 – FLYING WORKHORSE OF WW II is perfect for this book. The C-46 was very comparable to the C-47 in its expected duties except for its inability to land in the smaller fields like the C-47 could. The C-46 did however, carry larger loads and could fly higher altitudes than our C-47, so it did its assigned duties just as well! The C-47 was converted to wartime duty from the DC-3 that the Airlines used for a number of years. Many are still flying and, no doubt, some of you have been a passenger on the DC-3 sometime in the past.

Every plane in the skies in WW II was manufactured for a specific purpose. The Fighters were made to shoot down enemy fighters and to fly support for the Heavy Bomb Groups whose Bombers were made to drop heavy bomb loads from high altitudes. The Medium Bombers were made to carry lighter bomb loads, but could fly faster and bomb from lower altitudes. On many occasions, in fact, they were called upon to strafe a target from treetop level and the transports like the C-47 were called upon to do whatever was left to do. I don't mean to intimate that the C-47 was perhaps the only workhorse – but as a transport, it was expected to do more varied assignments.

That's pretty much what this book is about but I'm smart enough to realize that a book is not a book until some publisher says it's a book! Like George McGovern, it has to start earlier in life. Many interesting, as well as funny things happen in ones life worth sharing. Here's my share of history.

Lt. Richard D. Harvey

Chapter One

EARLY LIFE ON AN IOWA FARM AND THE DEPRESSION

As I begin this story I am reminded of an internationally known speaker who came to Chicago to address a large convention and when he had reached the podium, he looked out over a very large crowd, which startled him somewhat, and said, "Oh, my goodness! Where to start? Where to start?" Some wiseacre in the front row stood up and said, "Try to make it as close to the finish as you can!" That may not apply here but I know the feeling, where to start?

It would be difficult to start earlier than this. I was born May 28, 1919, on a farm five miles south of Williams, Iowa the last of nine children (five brothers and three sisters). When my dad saw me for the first time he probably said, "That's enough Eenie and Meanie, there ain't gonna be no Moe!" At that time, my dad was farming a rented half-section of good Iowa land. When I was old enough to understand, I was told that he had been doing pretty well as a farmer, with the help of my older brothers until he bought a bunch of cattle, hit a bad market and lost his shirt. I can believe that he was doing well at some point because in 1918 he bought a Lexington touring car. Even in those days it sold for about $1800.00. It was quite an automobile. I can only remember that we were poor although we still had the car. My brother, Jim, had a favorite saying, "We were so poor that we couldn't buy oats for a nightmare!" I didn't know what "nightmare" meant but I did understand poor. He had another saying about being poor, but I can't use it here! In spite of all that, we never went hungry. We did tire of beans and cornbread, however. My mother was a great cook, and could stretch a dollar farther than anyone I ever knew.

By the time I was old enough to go to country school, my oldest brother, Jess, had already enlisted in the Navy. He was quite a musician; in fact, I can remember the day his clarinet arrived in the mail; probably from Sears and Roebuck. He played in the shipboard band and continued his musical career later in life. Although I don't remember when Jess actually left for the Navy, I do remember when Tom, another brother, went into the Navy. He was not heavy enough on his first try but he came back to the farm and ate almost nothing but bananas for a short time. On his second attempt to enlist, he was accepted and made the Navy his life career, retiring in the early 1960's.

I finally reached school age and started to country school. My brother, Delbert, and I were the only ones in the family who were in school. We daily walked a little more than a mile each way, regardless of the weather. I recall my older siblings telling of going to country school when living on another farm. One day in early May, they had gone to school barefooted, and it snowed during the day. They had to walk home in the snow. On the farm, we were guilty of going barefoot just as quickly as the weather permitted – the first warm day! Those were days never to be forgotten and I think anyone who never had a country school experience missed an important part of life.

Many things happened in that old school more than I want to share, but I think it was in the second grade that I experienced my first love. Her name was Edna Knickerbocker. I can't remember whether the attraction was for Edna or the fact that her brother, Art, owned an airplane. They too were farmers and every so often Art would fly over the countryside and over our homestead. I knew nothing about airplanes, but it was always a thrill when he flew very low over our place. Even then, I never dreamed that I would ever ride in one much less fly one! Locked in my memory more than that, was the whuppin' I got in either the second or third grade. I had only indicated to a classmate how the teacher crossed her T's on the blackboard, which was across the top of the entire word. In any case, she saw me making the motion, hauled me off to the cloakroom, took down my pants (or overalls) and gave it to me on the bare rear with a ruler! I have often wondered, if this teacher isn't dead, if I could take her to court under today's rules. I am sure the ACLU would take up the wrong side. I think we would have a better school system today if we still allowed a whuppin-on-the-rear-end-with-a-ruler every time a student brought a gun to school. As many ornery things that I did in those days, the schoolhouse did burn down one winter night but I never got the blame for it. The teacher had banked the old pot-bellied stove with too much wood or coal, and it simply over-heated.

In either 1929 or 1930, the depression had come our way and we moved to Webster City, Iowa to a fifteen-acre place north of town. It had a nice sized house and because of the hard times some of my brothers moved back in (even a married one). All but my brother, Delbert, and I were fortunate to find jobs in town. In fact, at one time there were nine people

3

living in that house who went to work every day at the Knapp-Monarch factory where toasters and other small appliances were made. Everyone paid my mother room and board, we ate pretty well and everything was smooth sailing for the most part. Unfortunately my dad had to sell that Lexington automobile to a neighbor. He only managed to get $5.00 for that car and was lucky to get that much since times were tough. Had we been able to keep it later on as an antique, it would have been worth a fortune. In those days, you had to make do with what you had and hope for the best.

It was back to country school, a different one, for me. This school was also just over a mile each way like the first one. We walked it morning and night in all kinds of weather. My brother, Delbert, and I had to milk nine cows before school and the same nine cows after school. In looking back, it isn't difficult to see why I disliked the farm so much. I only attended that school through the eighth grade. Ultimately, so everyone could be closer to their jobs, we moved to town into a horrible house. It was so small - I think the landlord made it out of used orange crates. While I'm sure that isn't true, that's the way we always described it. In any case, it too was just about a mile walk to school. I started there in the ninth grade. My, what a change from country school! There must have been a tremendous change in me as well. How did I know that I would begin to notice the difference in the dresses that the girls and teachers wore in town school as opposed to the ones that were worn in country school? I came to the realization that it wasn't just the dresses. It seemed like it was a different bunch of bodies as well. Maybe too, it was because now, I was in the ninth grade - I had begun to notice things differently!

Not only was my homeroom teacher, Miss Halverson, very pretty but also she wore pretty clothes and she had a body that complimented every stitch. I tried every trick I knew and some new ones that I had learned, to try and get her to take me to the cloakroom and give it to me on the bare read-end. No luck! Had it happened I doubt that I would have felt a thing. (Gad, what a body!)

High school was a fun time because I made it a fun time. I enjoyed the fun a great deal more than I did the study and my grades showed it. I loved sports but I was too short (5' 5 ½") for basketball, and besides, I had to work in order to have any clothes or spending money. I carried papers in the ninth and tenth grades and worked for the Modern Cleaners and the Western Union on through high school. While carrying papers, I won a couple of air-rides for acquiring new customers. One ride was in an Autogyro (some of you can't even remember that one) and the other was in the old Ford Tri-motor. I can't remember much about the Autogyro ride but I'll never forget the Tri-motor. It rattled and shook like it was going to come apart in flight. Neither ride, as I recall, did much for my desire to fly.

I would have liked to play football but in spite of the work, I could never have made that team. I think our high school team could have beaten a number of college teams. In my senior year, the team scored 261 points in an eight game schedule, and was never scored upon! I only mention that because that record still stands there, and very few schools today could match that streak. I probably ought not to even mention this but I, along with another guy (Teeny Bringolf, who was killed in the war) and two girls, became the first cheerleading squad that the school ever had. It gave us an opportunity to attend all the games and we had a great time! I boxed for a short time to earn a little extra money. Only three round preliminaries with eight-ounce gloves prior to the main event. Some of you old-timers may remember the night that Tommy Farr fought Joe Louis to a fifteen round draw? I was on a card in Fort Dodge, Iowa. I drew an older "street fighter" and he turned me every way but loose. I got a cracked rib, crawled out from under the bottom rope, and that was the end of my boxing career. If you have ever had a cracked rib you know all about hurt.

As I said, high school was a fun time and I even learned how to date the girls. I think it was in my senior year that I was dating a Catholic girl and went to a Midnight Mass with her. I only mention this because it was the first time I was ever in a church, and it had some meaning later in life, which I will touch upon in another chapter.

During my senior year, we moved to a larger house which was much more livable. All of life is not a fun time. It was in that year that my mother lost two daughters in the same week. My sister, Carrie Pearl, died on a Sunday as a result of a car accident two years earlier that severed her spine. She was paralyzed from just below the shoulders. She caught the flu that was going around and died from it. For those two years, my mother cared for her in our home, a terrific burden on her but never a whimper. My sister, Lola, died from cancer on Thursday, leaving a husband and two small children. I have always marveled at my mother's courage and ability to handle such a tragedy, and without a whimper. Life is full of unscheduled tragedies, and should any occur to me, I only hope I can handle them as well as my mother.

There were fun times in that house in spite of the tragedy. My brother, Jess, the musical one along with another gentleman organized a fifteen piece dance band (and a darn good one!) and they would gather at our house and practice every week. They had a female singer and a male singer, as a part of the fifteen. Jess, played the sax, the clarinet, the violin, the guitar and the banjo. They bought those blank Mozart music books that Jess would use to arrange for every instrument in the band. An interesting side note: the leader, Al Havinga, who played the Accordion, was unable to play one night and Lawrence Welk took his place. This was during the time that Mr. Welk was at a radio station in Yankton, South Dakota long before anyone had ever heard of Lawrence Welk. Another brother of mine, Fred, also played a banjo in this band. In those hard times, instead of having contracts for a certain amount of money it was necessary to pass the hat, and hope for the best. Fred was in charge of counting and distributing the take and many times it consisted mostly of bottle caps. In spite of that they rather enjoyed it all. Today, quite often you hear someone say, "Give me the good old days!" That sure would be great but with today's appliances and salaries. (How would we get along without the "Boob Tube"?)

Chapter Two

SO NOW I'VE GRADUATED, WHAT'S NEXT?

I graduated on my eighteenth birthday with not a clue what life had in store for me. I had no money for college, although my boss at the cleaners indicated once that he would send me but quite frankly, I didn't think I had the smarts for college. In any case, I gave college no further thought. Shortly thereafter, I hitchhiked down to Decatur, Illinois and went to work in a factory, on the night shift, where my brother, Jim had been working for some time. I made better money, but I hated every minute of it. I had no friends there so it was just work nights and sleep days – what a life! I had an opportunity to return to the cleaners for $15.00 a week so I hitchhiked back home and went back to work at the cleaners as a heavy presser pressing men's clothes. I didn't mind the work but out of that $15.00 came the money I gave to my mother to help buy groceries so there wasn't a great deal left to buy clothes or for the fun things in life.

I started to date a farm girl, Marge Jewett; we went together for about thirteen months. She came from a very religious family, had gone to church and Sunday school all of her life. Quite frankly, I didn't know how that would all work out with my non-church background. However, I started going to church and Sunday school. I knew that I had to if anything was to come out of this relationship. I found it rather interesting, although I'm sure that I asked a lot of dumb and embarrassing questions. I found myself doubting a good share of the Bible but my attending church made me do a lot of outside study to try to dispel some of my doubts. That reading and digging for answers is still a great part of my life.

In early 1939, I asked Marge to marry me and by golly, she said yes - out of desperation I guess. We were both twenty years old and in my case, it was necessary for my dad to sign the marriage license. He worked about fourteen blocks from home, and without a car, I thought that was a long way to walk so I signed the license. I knew that it was illegal so I've always assumed that we were not legally married. I held that over my wife's head for the first five years of our marriage and she has held it over my head ever since! We were married on Thanksgiving, the 30th of November at 8:00 o'clock in the evening. I knew if the marriage was going to work, I would have to join the church so I was baptized in the First Christian Church and have continued to attend church regularly for the rest of our married lives (which was 64 years November of 2003). My boss gave me a $3.00 a week raise to $18.00 and Marge was working as a secretary at Beam Manufacturing, making $15.00 a week. We rented an upstairs apartment for $30.00 a month, bought furniture on time and also bought her wedding rings from a jeweler friend of mine for $25.00 and those too, were paid for on time. We had no automobile, walked to and from work, and thought we were sitting on top of the world! Money went a lot farther in 1939. Anyhow, we were living on love. Love costs a lot less now that we've been retired for over twenty years!

My father-in-law couldn't see putting out all that money for rent, so he gave us the money to buy a lot, and we built a five room bungalow with a full basement all for about $3,500.00. It was close to downtown and to work. We still didn't have a car, so we walked to and from work. I was thinking that we had bicycles but my wife just reminded me that we sold our bikes to get married so yes, we were still walking!

On Sunday, December 7, 1941, we were out at Marge's sister and brother-in-law's farm playing cards when we heard on the radio all about Pearl Harbor. We were shocked and found it hard to believe as everyone else in the world did too. I was never too good in geography so I never even knew where Pearl Harbor was. Needless to say, everyone in America very soon knew where it was. Very soon, we all knew what the draft was as well. I was eventually given a 3A classification in the draft, which only meant that I was married but had no children. We thought that I would eventually have to go into service. We gave it a lot of thought and we (or at least, I) decided that I would try to enlist in the Army Air Corps. At that point in life, it wasn't that I was so patriotic, although I wouldn't trade America for any other place that I have seen in my travels. Truthfully, I just didn't want to be in the walking Army if I could help it. As I have said many times, I learned to have the greatest respect for all the guys who fought the war in the trenches.

With that in mind, we quit our jobs and moved to California, thinking that I might get a job in an Aircraft Plant and get a good look at an airplane – just in case I did make it in the Air Corps. We got a room with a nice family on Vista Del Mar Street in Hollywood and started looking for jobs. I found out very quickly that I could not get a job in an Aircraft Plant (and I tried them all!) because I was 3A, but no children. They just wouldn't hire anyone with that classification. Jobs were plentiful and I got a job with Standard Oil, working in various oil stations all over Los Angeles. Most always it was at night, which meant that I would work until closing, lock up the station and then try to find the proper bus to get back to our room. What a miserable, miserable job! Although I did wait on one or two movie stars, John Paine, being one but even that didn't make the job any more favorable. I only worked a couple weeks at that job, and then I started looking in the want ads to find a job in what I knew best, pressing clothes.

Luckily, that job came along rather quickly. Foreman and Clark, a clothing store for men, advertised for an extra presser during the busy season pressing new clothes after alterations had been done. It was an easy job and paid pretty well. In the meantime, Marge had found a secretary's job in the Engineering Department for North American Aviation in El Segundo. With jobs, we started looking for an apartment, which we fortunately found on a short street named Cassel Place in downtown Hollywood between Hollywood and Sunset Boulevards. It was only four blocks to my job, and Marge found a ride with another who worked at North American, with her pick-up point not far from where we lived. I think we moved into that apartment on a Wednesday. We bought a few groceries to get us started and when we arrived at the apartment and checked our funds we didn't even have enough to write a letter home to borrow any money! However, we both had paychecks coming on Friday. We made out okay, but it was touch and go for a couple of days. We were young and didn't know any better. We frequently reminisce about those times in our lives. Can you imagine in today's world hitching a ride as Marge did, with a complete stranger that you had only met once? We get goose bumps just thinking about it.

We have laughed many times about the size of that apartment. It had one of those beds that folded up into the wall and when it was in the position for sleeping we could sit on one side of the bed and wash our feet in the toilet, and sit on the other side and cook our meals on a very small gas stove. Big, it wasn't. It was exciting to us and we enjoyed it. It was close to a lot of things in downtown Hollywood and without a car that meant a lot to us. We were able to take in some shows like the Lux Radio Theatre and the Bob Burns Show. That really dates us. I doubt if many can even remember Bob Burns and his Bazooka. It was cornball but funny. He also had Ginny Simms on his show. She was a singer in case you've forgotten! We danced to Harry James at the Palladium one time. Yes, there was a lot to enjoy in Hollywood at least in those days.

The California climate got to my wife, apparently, and she had become pregnant. We weren't looking for that at least not so quickly. In any case, we worked a short time longer and decided, due to the pregnancy, that we would be better off back in Webster City, Iowa so we left California and headed for home in June, 1942. This tidbit about the trip back to Webster City just dawned on me as I write this (and I had totally forgotten it!). I only mention it to show the difference in the times and in our thinking between the early 40's and now. We had very little money for a bus or train trip (and why we ever thought of this, I don't know!) but we checked the paper to find an advertisement for someone delivering an automobile back to the Midwest. There were several in the paper, so we chose one that would take us nearest to Webster City. If I remember correctly, the one that we chose went right through our hometown. We called the number in the ad, and fortunately, we were lucky to get a ride. What we didn't know at the time was that the driver had also promised three other men the same ride! The six of us piled into a 1939 or 1940 Chevrolet (I don't know where we put our luggage) and headed East for the 2300-mile trip. We drove straight through. Try to imagine today – one lady and four strange men that we had not met until we piled into that car! We made good time as I recall and arrived home safely. As we think about it in today's world we get goose bumps the size of warts! Soon after arriving back in Webster City, a friend and I went to Des Moines to take the test for the Air Cadet Program. The standards had been lowered; they needed pilots, bombardiers and navigators allowing non-college men to join the program. I barely passed and my friend just barely failed the test. We both were very disappointed because we thought that we would go to the Air Corps together. My wife was three months pregnant when I enlisted (and incidentally, that was not the reason I enlisted), but due to a shortage of training planes or instructors, I was not called until June of 1943. My son, Ron, was born in the meantime – a night that I have not forgotten. On December 6th, about three o'clock in the morning, my wife awakened me and said, "I think it's time." I almost fell out of bed but

13

I hurriedly got my clothes on, we still had no car, and in the freezing Iowa cold I ran about seven or eight blocks to my boss's house to borrow his car. When I got there I was sweating like a horse and almost stepped on my tongue! Everything worked out okay and we had our first of two sons. Our other son, Doug, was born on January 13th, 1948 after I returned from the war. We had a car by the time Doug came along but that's later in the story.

Not knowing for sure when my call for service would come, I had gone back to work at the cleaners to keep food on the table. I expected my call to be rather soon so I kept my teeth brushed and my bags packed. In the meantime, I was learning how to change diapers and bottle-feeding at two in the morning – boy was that fun!

Chapter Three

MY CALL TO THE ARMY AIR CORPS

I can't recall the exact date in June that my orders came or just how much time I had to report to San Antonio, Texas, to begin my next two and a half years in the United States Army Air Corps.

I said goodbye to my family and boarded the train in Iowa Falls, Iowa. Every stop the train made more men my age climbed on board. Each one of us knew, from our ages, that we had received the same orders and was heading to the same place. Consequently, new friendships were made even on the train. These were sad times, having said goodbye to our families, but at the same time, we were on a "high" because of expectations of what was to come.

After arriving in San Antonio, we were bussed or trucked to one of the many Service Installations, one being Classification, which was a series of meetings to make us aware of what was to come; the things we could and couldn't do in the Cadet Corps. This particular meeting I never will forget. We all were herded into an auditorium to hear about an hours worth of "do's and don'ts", finishing up with this dandy, "Don't ever come asking for a leave of absence because your wife is going to have a baby. You were there for the laying of the keel so you need not be there for the launching!" That's about as plain as one could put it and I doubt if we could have gotten leave to go home even for a death in the family. Thank God I never had to test it.

On the train to San Antonio, I met Les Buresh, from Mount Vernon, Iowa and Dale Griffith from Brooklyn, Iowa – two strangers that became good friends. Les was a poker buddy when we had the time. I mention his name for two reasons: I remember him walking about the base, constantly bringing up his right hand to touch the end of his nose with his finger trying to cross his eyes. Whatever the test was for, or whether he was ever able to accomplish it, I do not know. In any case, he eventually was sent to bombardier school in San Angelo, Texas. The second reason I mention his name is that when we parted company he owed me $20.00 from a poker debt. Having known him for such a short time I wasn't sure that I would ever see the $20.00 again although I had the feeling that I would. He came across as being a reliable type of guy and sure enough, out of our first paycheck I received the $20.00 in a letter. I mention Dale Griffith because he was a happy-go-lucky guy with a hitch in his get-along when he walked and just a fun, crazy guy to be around. For some reason I pinned the name "Buckshot" on him and it stuck throughout our training. One thing about the service, you met many great guys like Les and Buckshot. Occasionally, you'd run into one or two that you'd rather not be around, but that was the service. Most of the guys were great.

Classification had a number of functions. Initially, it gave us an opportunity to become acclimated to a completely different type of living than any of us were used to. In addition there were hours and hours of calisthenics, cross-country runs and more to get us in shape for what was to come. Many, many tests were given to determine exactly where we would best fit into the Corps. I had only one ambition and that was to become a pilot. I gave no thought at all to becoming a bombardier or a navigator, only a pilot. I remember some of the tests, and as I recall, the Depth Perception test was very critical to becoming a pilot. I was never exposed to the "cross-your-eyes" test that Les had the difficulty with. The word mechanical was thrown at us quite often. If you were too mechanical, you would more than likely wash out. I never really knew just what that meant. I finally came to the conclusion that your instructor could tell if you had a feel for the airplane. I might describe it as a flying-by-the-seat-of-your-pants; in any case I apparently wasn't mechanical.

Speaking of becoming a pilot, and I can't explain this, but I'm scared to death of heights. I remember when I took the Air Corps test while back in Des Moines; we had some extra time so we toured the state capitol building. As I remember, you can go as high as the fifth floor and still look down into the atrium and see the ground floor. I crawled up to the railing on my hands and knees in order to look over the edge. I luckily never had this feeling in an airplane. I think what got me so eager to become a pilot was when the P-38 came along. I thought that was the sharpest airplane I had ever seen and could visualize taking Primary, Basic and Advanced training in the P-38 and then flying it in combat – but that's another story.

When we finished Classification, those who hadn't "washed-out" for whatever reason, just moved across the road for Preflight training. Some of the others were sent elsewhere, perhaps for bombardier or navigator training.

Preflight still necessitated a lot of calisthenics and cross-county runs to keep us in shape. The major emphasis, however, was on a lot of ground school. I soon found out why they would rather have had the college guys, yes, it was difficult for me, but somehow I got through it okay. The worst thing about Preflight and believe me, Preflight was bad, was that we were subject to a 'Class System'. Most of us had no inkling that it existed. I thought it was stupid at the outset and I have not changed my mind one iota. I was never able to figure out the need for it, although I think it is still a part of West Point, The Naval Academy and the Air Force Academy so there must be a legitimate reason for it.

I mentioned earlier that I hadn't had any church experience until marriage and I had not learned to think about or to give any credence to a God. I only mention that here because as I have grown older and been very active in the various churches that we have belonged to in our marriage I am convinced, as I look back over my time in service that without realizing it, God had His hand on my shoulder many times. I will refer to those times as I go along. Undoubtedly, my first unknown experience was when He guided me to Marge and to our marriage because she has been responsible for my becoming active in church, which in turn has made me dig, read and study in my spiritual walk. Without realizing it then, I think God had a hand in directing me to the Air Corps. As I look back now, I am satisfied that is where I belonged.

The Class System was set up so that each of us was assigned a bay on the ground floor. Immediately above us on the second floor in the same location was an upper classman, who then became our mentor and counselor. Many, or perhaps I should say most of the upper classmen were from another planet or at least I thought so. They really made it miserable for us lower classmen. Again, unbeknownst to me, God intervened once again and put me in a bay downstairs from Big George Kuklinski from West Allis, Wisconsin who then became my mentor. I remember the very first night, after running our tails off the entire day and being yelled at constantly by the upper classmen I was ready to tell somebody to "shove it" and head for the walking army. There I was, twenty-three years old, lying in bed and crying like a baby. What in the hell have I gotten myself into I thought? In any case, Big George came down that night and said to me, "It's going to be rough but don't let these nuts get to you. It will all work out." Thanks to Big George! I am sure he felt the same way as I did about the Class System. As difficult as Preflight was there were at least two occurrences that will be engrained forever in my mind. First, our class was the last of the Class System in the Army Air Corps. It was discontinued for whatever reason and that was a good thing, because some of the new class who would have been our under classmen had come back from overseas to go through flight training. Under no circumstance would those guys have put up with the garbage that had been thrown at us. The second thing was one of the funnier moments that happened to me during my time in the service. It was the only time that I ever drew guard duty in my life. It must have been on the same field where we did our daily calisthenics. It seems that I started at the corner of a building, walked about 30 or 40 paces to an imaginary point and then walked about the same number of paces to the edge of this dirt field. It was at night, coal black out and I was walking with a wooden gun. I had just gotten to the first point when I heard someone coming. I shouted the customary, "Who goes there?" He answered something and then I said, "Advance two steps and drop your name tags," which he did. I started scratching around in the dirt looking for those tags. Next thing I knew both of us were down on our knees, nose to nose looking for those tags. One of us finally found the tags; he put them back on and went on his merry way - laughing probably, but I never heard him. What an experience but I have had a lot of laughs over it myself. Thank the Good Lord that he wasn't an enemy or an upper classman – in my mind, they were two-of-a-kind!

When we became upper classmen - thank God when that happened - the remaining time in Preflight was uneventful without that dreaded Class System. We had been so looking forward to Preflight training because Classification had become boring. Preflight was never boring – too much to do!

In spite of our continued calisthenics and increased ground school, we seemed to have a little more time to ourselves. Preflight was not easy, but we took it day-by-day, doing the best we could and hoping for the best.

As anyone who has been in the service can attest to, you become better acquainted with those who were close to you alphabetically. That's where Jack Gish, from Omaha, Nebraska, comes in. Let me say first that there were a number of times when we were given an opportunity to volunteer for something and it was a way to break the monotony sometimes.

On this particular day they had asked if anyone would be interested in going to experience an oxygen chamber. Quite a few volunteered, which included both Jack and me. We sat down in that chamber and as I recall, Jack was sitting across from me. We each were given a tablet of paper and a pencil. We were to write whatever came to mind on that tablet and they could tell from your writing when you needed the oxygen mask put on. I think at about 20,000 feet, Jack threw up in his mask that had been put on earlier. I was so busy writing, "P--s on the upper classmen! P--s on the upper classmen! P--s on the upper classmen!" that I don't remember what they did with Jack. Probably took him out of the chamber and cleaned him up. I had written those three lines on my tablet – the first line straight across the page, the second line went down the page and out about half way down the page and the third line was not at all legible and nearly went off the bottom of the page. At 28,000 feet they put my mask on and almost immediately things were back to normal. As I think back on that experience, for anyone who is contemplating suicide, that's the way to do it. You're breathing normally just not getting any oxygen. You feel like you're on a two day drunk and you could care less. No pain and very shortly you're no longer among the living. I'm not suggesting it by any means!

Close to me in class alphabetically was Frank Harvey (no relation), from Kansas. Frank had just failed a Morse code test at a very critical point in our training. When it was time to go on to the next training period, Primary, many of us wanted to move out together. This was one of the dumbest things I ever did in the service but Frank and I got our heads together and thought we'd figured out a way where I could take the test and he would turn it in as his. We took the test all right and got caught. That kind of thing is against the Cadet Code of Ethics and was an automatic "wash out". No questions asked; you're gone! God was looking over both of our shoulders because the instructor gave us a good talking to and made Frank take the test over again and this time he passed. I've always been told that God works in strange ways. In any case, nothing else was ever said about it but I think both Frank and I learned what could have been a most costly lesson.

Finally, all the tests were done and we were ready for the next phase of training. It was a time that we had worked so hard for and had all been looking forward to so very much but it was a sad day as well. The close friends that we had made in the class would now be sent to different locations never to see each other again in the service. I went to pilot training along with several others, some went to bombardier training, some went to navigator training and a good many just plain washed out. It wasn't difficult to figure out who had washed out – the long faces told the story. I felt so very sorry for those who had washed out because they were just as determined to be somewhere in the air as the rest of us but it just wasn't to be. Virg Haldeen, from Sterling, Colorado and his wife had become very good friends with my wife and me. He never made it and he was so set on becoming a pilot. I felt so sorry for him. What he finally became I don't remember but he survived the war and we later went to visit him. I think he was running a restaurant in Sterling. Some ended up as gunners, others as radio specialists or crew chiefs but at least they were flying. Many may have ended up somewhere on the ground because the wash out percentage was pretty high as it was in most every class that went through Classification and Preflight.

I think by this time most of us had become acclimated to Air Corps life, what was expected or what we could and couldn't do. The "White Glove" treatment was always surprising, barracks inspections, the God-awful, every morning reveilles, when we were half asleep. Not to mention the Saturday morning 'dressed' inspections, as we stood in the Texas heat. Many times during those inspections we could see one fellow drop here and another drop there from the heat, all while standing at attention. Everyone in service had to put up with that and we were no better than anyone else.

Chapter Four

FINALLY, OFF TO FLYING SCHOOL

I, along with some new-made friends was sent to Corsicana, Texas for single engine primary training. It was an exciting time for all of us, even before we had seen the PT-19 that would be our trainer. As I recall, and I was never able to figure out why, but we were lined up according to height and I was only five feet five and a half inches tall and all of the seven or eight Cadets that were assigned to a certain instructor were about the same height. Even our instructor was as short as we were. I remember that he was from Des Moines, Iowa, but I can't recall his name. The PT-19 was a good airplane for training and I was looking forward to my first flight. However, it didn't turn out quite like I expected it. I got airsick and threw up all over the cockpit. When that happens, it is the responsibility of the thrower-upper to clean it all up, which I reluctantly did. The same thing happened on the second flight and the third flight. I figured then that if I didn't make it as a pilot, with my experience I would have no equal at cleaning up airplanes. It never happened again my entire time in training or after I got my wings. They told me that this problem is caused by fear that you're not even aware of. I can't argue that point!

Corsicana was a decent and friendly community with not many service people. In San Antonio, we were told there were over 1,000,000 service people in the city. As I recall, there were eight or nine military installations in San Antonio. It surely seemed that way when we had an opportunity to go to town. I think that is why we were so glad to get to a smaller community like Corsicana.

The PT-19 was easy and fun to fly although I remember a number of center sections were broken from dropping in for a landing from too high an altitude. That is where your depth perception comes into play. I really never had any difficulty in Primary although I became aware very quickly that I would never be a fighter pilot. I was unable do the various maneuvers that were necessary. I just couldn't manage any maneuver that necessitated a fully extended right arm along with a fully extended left leg. My instructor finally told me to never go to the flight line without two pillows to put behind my back. They were about three feet long and perhaps two feet wide and about five inches thick. From then on, I used the two behind my back so I could reach everything. Needless to say, I received a lot of kidding about the pillows but my instructor was the boss! I wasn't even disappointed when I knew that I would never become a fighter pilot, except that the P-38 was now just a memory. Maybe God had a hand in that too though the other cadets were just as short as I was and they seemed to get along okay. When I discovered that I couldn't do the maneuvers properly, I planned then to request whatever flying was straight and level, but that will come later. Nothing spectacular happened during Primary and when we finally finished training, our instructor had a party at his home. He had a washtub full of iced home brew. Although I'm not a beer drinker, I had learned to like home brew because my dad always had some brewing growing up on the farm. We may have become a bit limber that night, letting our hair down and during that time my instructor told me that I had never had a pink slip (this is something issued for a bad flight). That surprised me somewhat because as much as I had looked forward to flying it never bothered me when we were rained out. Then too, I wondered about my bad maneuvers?

After Primary, it was on to Greenville, Texas, for Basic training in the BT-13 better known as the 'Vultee Vibrator'. It had an engine with much more power than the PT-19. As a result of the power it was more fun to fly. I was able to do most of the maneuvers except the slow roll. I never did master that but when trying to do the slow roll I perfected the Split S maneuver better than anyone else in fact it was the only maneuver that I really mastered! Anyone in flying knows that the Split S is the result of botching the slow roll and is not particularly a feather in one's hat! I really don't remember much about Basic training except that it was more fun than Primary. We were learning more about the feel of an airplane; more schooling and I think we learned how to use the E6B computer and cross-country flying. There is no better place to learn to fly than flat Texas. We were always reminded by our instructor to keep a constant eye out for a landing place in case of an emergency. I never worried much about that because from the air, Texas looks like a never-ending landing field. Cross-countries were fun that is if you didn't get lost. I imagine that all of us got lost at least once. My Basic training instructor was Lieutenant Hersan. I don't remember much about him so he must have been a decent and likable person. Had he been chicken-shit, as some were, I would have remembered that. Somewhere along the line, either in Primary or Basic, cadet officers were elected. Someone entered my name for consideration, and I don't know why, because no one knew me, at least not for very long. I was elected along with Chuck Healy, probably my best friend in training. Chuck was a Group II Commander and I was a Squadron Commander. I don't recall what our duties were but for whatever reason, we were put together in student officer's quarters that were separate from the rest of the cadets. I think we were to be role models making all formations on time and adhering to cadet rules. Both of us were Class 44-A, which meant if we didn't wash out we would graduate as Second Lieutenants in January of 1944. It was a goal that we all wanted to achieve and worked so hard toward. I can't remember that Basic training produced any memorable events other than just the regular routine of learning more and more about flying. Sometimes funny things happen that remain in our memories. One that I fondly recall involved Dale Griffith whom I'd met earlier on the train to San Antonio and was still with me in Basic training. All cadets nearly always had upper and lower bunks everywhere we were and I always tried to get an upper. Both Dale and I had upper bunks and the beds were very close together. Dale dreamt one night that he was in a spin and fell out of the upper bunk – ker whompf!- he landed on the floor waking up about half of the barracks. It could only happen to 'Buckshot'. We parted ways after Basic and I think he eventually became a fighter pilot. I know that he survived the war and was back in Brooklyn, Iowa. He was a funny guy to be around.

The God-awful noise the BT-13 made when taking off was something that stayed with me. I think it had a 450 horsepower engine and it was noisy. We were in Wichita, Kansas one time, probably on a cross-country trip, on a field where B-29's were stationed. I was in the number one position for take-off behind a B-29 taking off. That BT-13 made more noise with one engine than the B-29 did with all four! Another memory of the BT-13 is, in fact, (I'm sure that every cadet remembered the first time he did a stall) – it would begin to shake and shudder like it was about to take its last breath. Obviously, that's where it got its name, 'Vultee Vibrator'. Another maneuver that I was never able to accomplish was an Immelmann Turn. That's where a half loop and then a half a roll are completed in order to simultaneously gain altitude and change direction. I just couldn't seem to do the half-roll on top of the loop. Guess I was just built too short but being short might have been a lifesaver. I think it was in Basic that we had to make a choice: fighters or bombers and since I couldn't do some necessary maneuvers, I thought it was straight and level flying for me so I chose the B-24. More about that at a later time. Once again, it meant separation from new-made friends. Some would continue in single engine training while the rest of us would go to multi-engine training. My next move was to Frederick, Oklahoma for twin-engine UC-78 training.

In thumbing through the class book from Basic training I ran across this poem written by R.L. Sterba, entitled "The Call Skyward". It's worth sharing.

The call of the sky is the call of the brave, the call of the young and the true.

It's a call of the wind, a call of the clouds, a call of the infinite blue.

It's a call to challenge the fates of old, and soar through the great unknown,

To free the spirit and right the wrongs the fears that men have sown.

There are some that answer whose skin is dark, and some whose skin is fair,

From farm and city, forest and vale, now brothers of the air.

Their eyes are bright, their voice is clear; their clasp is warm and strong.

It's the brave that answer, the brave that go where only the brave belong.

So if you are honored to hear the call and feel the sky in your heart,

Be quick to answer, eager to learn and ready to play your part.

Ready to fly with the dove of peace, and to dive with the eagles of war.

Once you've tasted the thrill of the sky, you're an airman evermore.

And when towards the end of your well-flown flight, you near the celestial field,

And the lights blaze out to show the way with the glories of heav'n revealed;

When your Commander's voice rings through the air, above your engine's purr,

With record clean, you can say, "Reporting as ordered, sir."

That's a good spot to leave Basic and on to Frederick, Oklahoma for Advanced training. Again, good friends were to separate. Some would continue on in single engine to become fighter pilots, and the rest of us to twin engine to become bomber pilots or wherever needed, and multi-engine would direct. This was really the training period that we were looking forward to. Number one, we had a better knowledge of flying and secondly, at the end of this period, we would get our Wings and Commission. What would come after that, only God and the Air Force would know!

I think I lucked out again. My instructor was Lt. Harvey Crumm from Texas. He was an all business, no nonsense good instructor. I don't recall ever hearing him eat out a cadet for some wrongdoing. The UC-78 was an easy airplane to fly except when you wanted to make a three-point landing. That was a bit tricky. We had already tasted formation flying but not quite like what we were going to do in Advanced. We were taught how to fly a tighter formation and that did come in handy later on down the road. We really used the E6B computer here and did a lot of cross-country flying. I remember one cross-country problem that we were given that had to be worked out on the E6B. I don't remember exactly what we had to do but I think we were given a specific cross-country route to fly. We were given our instructor's take-off time and when he would be at an imaginary point and we were to arrive at that point at the same time that he did. We worked out the problem on the E6B and took off at the worked out time. I flew the assigned cross-country, and when I reached that certain point, which might have been a town water-tank or an oil derrick, something recognizable at the specified time, I did a 90 degree left turn and fell right in on my instructor's left wing. I probably couldn't have done that again in a million years! We never had to do it again, thank God.

Everything that we were assigned to do didn't always turn out so well. I remember (how could I forget) one night when we were just shooting touch-and-go landings on some auxiliary fields around Frederick. There would be an instructor sitting in a UC-78 on a given field to give landing instructions. Incidentally, those were night landings. I had called for instructions and once they were given I then proceeded to land or touch-and-go but to my surprise when I landed, there wasn't another plane on the field. I had landed on the wrong field! I took off again, found the right field and landed and not one word was ever said about it. I sweat that one out!

Another time all of the cadets were flying night cross-countries when Frederick, Oklahoma got weathered in. We desperately had to find some auxiliary fields to land in before we ran out of fuel. A number of us made it to Clarendon, Texas and some even went as far as Amarillo. We stayed in various places in the airplanes until the weather cleared so we could return to Frederick. Those of us, who had enough fuel to return, did so. Some didn't have enough fuel so they hooked a ride back to Frederick with some of us. We flew back the next day to bring back the airplanes with low fuel. We had to siphon fuel from our planes to put into the others to return to Frederick. There were some close calls that day. One of the cadets reached Frederick okay and when he landed on the wheels and the tail wheel lowered to the ground, he had no more fuel. They came out with a vehicle and pulled him to the parking area. Even I had a little difficulty. I ran into a terrible sand storm, which knocked out the radio, the only way to find the home tower. I got down as close as I could to the ground and I spotted a large metal shed with Snyder painted on the roof. I knew then that I was just a short distance north of the home field. I just followed the highway that took me right into Frederick, landed the plane, breathed a sigh of relief and went on with living.

Throughout the training in Advanced, we felt pretty secure in our flying ability. Our training consisted of many cross-countries, formation flying, particularly night formation that was not fun really and still a lot of calisthenics to keep us in shape. We managed to finish Advanced without any accidents and were looking forward to graduation, getting Wings and Commissions, and getting on to our next assignments again, without a clue of what was in store.

This was what it was all about! This made it all worthwhile! The enlisting, the being away from home, the Class System, all the flying that was crammed into such a short period of time, those cherished Wings and a Lieutenant Commission, that earlier on, I perhaps only dreamed could happen. All the above is true even the dreaming but sometimes, when you least expect it, you get a touch of reality! Let me share "reality". Chuck Healy, whom I mentioned before remained with me all through training. His wife Donna and my wife, Marge came down for our graduation. Chuck and I, for whatever reason, a couple of days before the big day, purposely missed a formation to do something with our wives that we thought was more important. Well, Lt. Ed Clark, a Tactical Officer (those who keep the cadets in line) thought otherwise when he found out that we had missed the formation. I don't recall what was done to Chuck, but I got fifteen "tours". I seem to have forgotten exactly what a tour entailed, but if memory serves me, I believe it involved walking up and down in front of the Administration Building with a wooden gun for a certain amount of time. Most of the Tac Officers had been washed-out cadets, so we were told, and when they could make an example out of a cadet for any infraction that's how they got their jollies. Remember, we were only a couple of days from becoming Commissioned Officers. I stood before Lt. Clark at his desk and he said to me, "You're gonna walk those tours whether you walk them as a cadet or as an Officer!" and so I did. Since both Chuck and I were class officers ever since Primary training, we certainly weren't supposed to miss any formations, and I am sure that is the only formation that either of us missed all through training. That's something that a person should learn early in Service. If you need to please your wife, or, Uncle Sam – it better be Uncle Sam!

Chapter Five

AFTER GRADUATION – WHAT'S NEXT?

Yes, in spite of the tours, graduation day was going to be quite a day for a green, Iowa farm boy! My wife and I had rented a room from some nice folks and another cadet, A.J. Harris and his wife, also rented a room there. The entire 44-A class was to get a one-week leave to go home. Well, A.J. and I got snowed in along with a lot of others, and were unable to get out of Frederick until the next day. We were terribly low on money and when we had to stay the extra day, I spent most of my money for the ingredients to make a macaroni casserole dish that Marge and I like – easy to make and it went a long way. When we sat down to eat, I remember A.J., who was from Texas, saying, "It's not bad for a Yankee dish!" Whether he was kidding or not, I never found out. The next day we went our separate ways and I never saw the Harris's again.

I can't remember when I received my next orders but I soon knew that I was not going to B-24 training as a number of my classmates had. I was assigned to Randolph Field in San Antonio, Texas, for thirty days training to become an instructor. In those 30 days, as a class, we got only ten hours of flight time. The weather was unusually bad for Texas and we just couldn't get into the air. I don't remember what else we went through there, but at the end of the 30 days, I returned to Frederick as a twin-engine instructor. Needless to say, I wasn't very happy the way things turned out but then, I think maybe God had His hand in my life again. I really wanted that B-24, but later on in the war, I came to the conclusion that I was pretty lucky the way it all worked out. I'll touch on that later in another chapter.

My wife and son, Ron, came down; we had rented a house and I began my new duty. As I think back, that would have been decent duty for the remainder of the war, but it just wasn't meant to be. More on this later. It was enjoyable, meeting the new cadets in each class, and watching their development during training. There were some things that stuck in my memory. One of my cadets and I were just shooting touch-and-go landings at an auxiliary field and when we were on the final approach to landing, I said to him, "Haven't you forgotten something?" He had forgotten to put the wheels down, so, around we went again and so help me, he forgot them again so, around we went again and this time he remembered. I never wrote a report on him and he turned out to be a decent pilot. Another interesting thing happened after a cadet cross-country one night. At about 1:00 o'clock in the morning this cadet was on the downwind side of the landing pattern (as it sometimes happened, his pattern was far to far out). We were always told that the downwind leg of the pattern was supposed to be close enough to the field that if trouble developed, you could turn right into the field and make a landing. In any case, his pattern was too far from the field and he did run out of gas. He was in touch with the tower who had him in sight by the lights on the plane, he was a cool individual, and all he did was to trim it just above stalling speed and flew it in. God must have had a hand in this one as well. The cadet landed in a barnyard, the tail wheel catching on a barbwire fence, the right wing tip hit the corner of the barn, and he slid to a stop. When they went to find him in a Jeep, he was sitting out on the wing waiting for a pick-up. One of the lights was still on in the plane, which helped to find him. He wasn't one of my cadets so I don't know why I was selected to give him a check ride before he could get back into training. He was still a cool individual and had no problem at all with the check ride. He was about six foot two inches and I didn't have a clue where he ended up but I would bet flying either B-17's or B-24's.

One afternoon, Major White, the Air Inspector on the field was out on a flight and had to go, and you know – when you gotta go, you gotta go. There were relief tubes under the pilot's seat for that occasion, but when he reached down to pull it up into position, it was wired to the floor. This particular plane had come to our field from Sweetwater, Texas, where the women pilots were being trained. If it had been me I would have been looking for a flat spot to land. Major White made out just fine in the end I'm sure!

I've been reminded of this memory a good many times. As an instructor, we were allowed to take our wives up in the plane only one time. I took my wife up for that ride and showed her a little bit of Oklahoma from the air. When I came into land I intended to three point the landing, then I got to thinking how easy it was not to make a good landing so I decided to land only on the wheels with the tail up. When I pushed forward on the wheel, they hit the runway and we bounced about five or six times. I was embarrassed and it goes without saying that I've never heard the last of that story! God must have been out to lunch!

One of the scariest things as an instructor is to teach cadets night formation. At that time in their training, they think they are pretty good pilots (I know this because I thought the same thing as a cadet) and they like to fly a tighter formation than called for. We usually had seven or eight cadets of our own to check out in formation flying and some of the older instructors would sit in the ready room and watch "girlie" films while we new instructors checked out their cadets as well. I didn't think it was right and I said too many words to that effect to a Major, who was a Squadron Commander, and in two weeks I had orders to go overseas. As it all turned out, maybe God had a hand in that too. My mouthing off may not have had a thing to do with my going overseas, because a number of the instructors were sent out at the same time but to different locations overseas.

Chapter Six

ON OUR WAY OVERSEAS BUT TO WHERE?

I think this was a time we all knew would happen sometime in our service career but how do you prepare, mentally, for going to God knows where and for how long and worst of all, would we come back? Leaving one's family was not the easiest thing in the world but we all were in the same boat. We tried not to dwell on that, but learned to take things in stride, do what we were trained to do and hope for the best.

We said our goodbyes to our families and headed for Greensboro, North Carolina. I don't remember how long we were there or just why we were there, probably shots and the customary preparing for going overseas. We eventually headed for Hampton Roads, Virginia where we boarded a Liberty ship. As I recall there were only about thirty officers, most of them pilots, on board this ship. We had pretty good quarters and the food was great. We eventually joined a convoy of ships (80 total) and headed for – we never had a clue where we were going or what we had been assigned to. You can bet that we spent many hours with each other in conjecture and speculation and I doubt if anyone of us ever got very close to reality. I certainly did not!

One night we were attacked as we moved through the Straights of Gibraltar. Along with our machine guns, we had a number of five or six inch guns on our ship, as did some of the other ships. Everything opened up on some of the ships. Another fellow and I went up on deck and hunched down behind a tank that was fastened down on the deck.

The machine gun tracers were going over very low across our deck and the big guns were really making a racket. I never heard any airplanes at anytime and I have always thought it was just a mock raid of some sort just to give us a feel of, what I could envision, might sometime be ahead of us. Nothing was ever mentioned about it so I don't know if I was right, although it is hard to believe something like that would be staged. I was probably wrong!

The entire trip was forty-five long days, fifteen of which were spent in Bizerte, North Africa. While in Bizerte some of the guys (who had more guts than I and were better swimmers) dove off the side of the ship into the blue Mediterranean Sea. I watched for a while then went down a ladder about half way and jumped after I had thrown a life preserver into the water. As I began to swim out after the life preserver the waves were taking it out faster than I could swim to catch it. Desperately, I finally caught up with it, hung on for dear life and swam right back to the ship where I scrambled up the ladder and never tried that stunt again!

Two or three days before D-Day (June 6) we watched a procession of every kind of ship imaginable go by just barely in sight. We obviously didn't know what was going on but they must have been a part of the Normandy Invasion. We finally left Bizerte and in a few days disembarked from our "forty-five-day-all-expense-paid-pleasure-cruise" into the harbor of Taranto, Italy, which is high up the inside of the heel of Italy. We were quickly picked up in trucks and taken directly across the country to Brindisi, Italy on the coast of the Adriatic Sea.

It was good to have our feet on solid ground even in southern Italy. Though we spent fifteen days at Bizerte, we never got to go into the city and I doubt that we missed very much. The ship's officers went into town at least once because I remember the Captain of the ship, who normally wore a Lieutenant Colonel's Rank, wore a Full Colonel's Rank that day. It could have been perfectly legitimate, having gotten a promotion aboard ship. Those are Ranks that I'm familiar with and if they were Navy Ranks, I don't know what they were called.

I'd like to share the inception and some of the history of the 60th Troop Carrier Group, since it would be my home away from home for the remainder of the war. I have taken this information from a *Memoirs* journal about the 12th Squadron specifically. Fourteen officers and enlisted men put this *Memoirs* journal together while we were still in Brindisi. It is a fantastic depiction of life in the 12th Squadron.

Chapter Seven

THE HISTORY OF THE 60ᵀᴴ TROOP CARRIER GROUP

Director – Captain Max Goldschlag, Editor – S/Sgt. William J. Fraser, Biographical Sketches – 1ˢᵗ Lt. Wilmer E. Bratton and T/Sgt. Louis Sweet (who conceived the original idea of this journal), Technical Assistance – 1ˢᵗ Sgt. William Gaskill and Cpl. Leo Greenbaum, Artwork – Cpl. John J. Donovan and Pfc. Andrew S. Dagosta, Photography – T/Sgt. Robert Miley, S/Sgt. Samuel Monsoor and S/Sgt, George A. Stefura, Awards and Decorations – Sgt. Harold C. Way, Memoriam Page and Addresses – S/Sgt. James J. Graham, Jr. and Sgt. John J. Blake. The journal committee acknowledges its gratitude to the following men for their valuable assistance in the preparation of this journal but who were not able to be with us at publishing time. Those injured in plane crashes were Sgt. George C. Fernback and Lt. Edmond A Marquis.

Foreword

A suggestion made during a general Squadron meeting resulted in the publishing of this journal for you. Together we have gone through a great deal. There have been days of sunshine and days of cloudy weather. There are incidents that we will never forget. May this journal play a part in helping to keep those memories of life in the 12ᵗʰ Squadron intact.

SQUADRON HISTORY IN THE UNITED STATES

The 12th Transport Squadron, which was later to become the 12th Troop Carrier Squadron, was born on December 1, 1940 and was at best a very puny infant. First Lt. Arthur L. Logan was appointed Commander of the Squadron, but all that appointment entailed was the title, for the Squadron had no men, equipment or airplanes. The Squadron remained an organization in name only until February 1, 1941 when sixty-seven enlisted men were suddenly assigned. A great many of these enlisted men remained with the Squadron all through its long and eventful career, and many of them will probably remain with it for as long as it exists. Most of those who remain have risen to positions of responsibility, either as officers or as high-ranking enlisted men. Many have been returned to the United States in the past year, but if we were to judge by their letters they would very much like to be back with the 12th.

With the arrival of these first men, the name 12th Transport Squadron took on definite meaning. There wasn't much work to be done in the Squadron itself for there were still no airplanes, hangars or separate quarters assigned to the organization. The men worked with other Transport Squadrons and with the base unit on the field. All wasn't work, however, and the town and cities near the Middletown Air Depot were friendly to soldiers. Willow's Dance Hall and the Blue Room Café became the Squadron's unofficial headquarters, and are still talked about glowingly when conversation turns to reminiscing. The Hershey Chocolate Company opened its doors and its heart to our men and provided them with an amusement park, swimming pool, and open-air dance hall. War was still far away then and the times were good for soldiers.

It was a sad day when the Squadron received orders to move to Mitchel Field, Long Island, but the prospect of being stationed close to New York City went a long way toward relieving the gloom. Motor convoy made the move, and the fact that the road between Middletown and Mitchel wasn't strewn with the wrecks of civilian cars is a tribute to the luck of the civilian drivers. The move served to cement the Squadron into a solid unit and from that day on it became an organization that its members could be proud of. First Lt. Gregory F. Keenan had taken command of the Squadron just prior to the move and he commended us on the speed and efficiency with which the move had been accomplished.

We were pleasantly surprised, when we arrived at our destination, to find that Mitchel Field was a beautiful, modern post, and even more surprised when we were assigned to a newly developed area not very far from the hangars and the line soon after our arrival there. We had three barracks, a dayroom, and an orderly room, and there was ample space for the number of men in the Squadron at that time. We soon found that we were going to spend only a minimum of time in our Squadron area however, for the people in the vicinity of the field were as anxious to entertain the soldiers as the people around Middletown had been. It was a common sight to see a limousine with a liveried chauffeur at the wheel pull up at the gates and pick up a soldier. We went social in a big way, and Emily Post's book became the most popular reading matter in the Squadron. Squadron social activities weren't neglected however, and one beach party is still remembered vividly. It was held at Jones' Beach on Long Island, one fine summer day. Plenty of food and drink was available and we made short work of it all. Everyone went swimming whether they wanted to or not, and whether they were dressed for swimming or not. A few free-for-alls at the end of the day made the party complete.

It was on August 5th that the Squadron really became an air-corps unit. Lt. Keenan brought in a brand new Douglas C-53, and our mechanics, who had been occupying themselves by seeing how clean they could get the hangar floor, swarmed all over it. That the airplane survived that first onslaught is still considered something of a miracle. Soon after the arrival of our first airplane, we received more additions to the Squadron. Thirty or forty selective service men were assigned, and were subjected to the usual recruit hazing. They quickly became an integral part of the Squadron however, and the stigma of "draftees" was soon forgotten. Many more draftees were assigned in the next few months as well as two more airplanes and we were very proud of the fact that we were successful in keeping three transports flying. We didn't suspect that within a short amount of time we would be keeping thirteen of them flying with practically the same number of men.

When war came on December 7th we hardly realized what it would eventually mean to us. Only after some time did the full significance of our country's declaration of war penetrate our minds. There was an air-raid scare soon after December

7th, and it was noteworthy in that is showed us how little prepared for war we were. When the alarm sounded, we were all roused out of the barracks and into a formation in the company street. No one was quite sure what should be done, so we merely stood there in nice straight lines until the all clear sounded. Many of us have since speculated on what would have happened then had there actually been an attack on the field.

Within a week the Squadron was alerted for movement, and a few days later we were on our way. The movement was the first one we ever made by air. Our new base was Westover Field in Massachusetts, and it didn't take us long to make ourselves comfortable. The entire 60th Transport Group was stationed at Westover, and a strenuous training program was immediately undertaken. Lt. Gordon L. Edris had assumed command of the Squadron when we moved, and to him fell the job of making the Squadron conform to the high standards set by Col. Maughan who was then Group Commander, and later to those set by Col. Malone who succeeded Col. Maughan.

The pre-war, carefree days were over. We never realized it more than when we heard that all Christmas and New Years furloughs had been cancelled. Passes were limited to thirty-six hours, and only 20 percent of the Squadron could be absent at any time. Despite these restrictions we became well known in the towns adjoining the field. The Wonder Bar and Hotel Worthy in Springfield, and the Roger Smith Hotel in Holyoke were the gay spots that the 12th helped to make gayer. Christmas and New Years were dreary times for most of us, but a few of the luckier men managed to secure thirty-six hour passes. Many of us lived within a hundred miles or so of the base, and it was terribly hard to sit in the barracks on Christmas and New Years Eves visualizing what our loved ones at home were doing, when we could have been with them in such a short time had we been allowed to leave the post. The intensive training program went on through the following months. Then in March we received a shock. Our outfit was suddenly split up, and half of it left for Pope Field, North Carolina to form a Ferry Squadron. Old friends were separated, and men flew everywhere either trying to be among those leaving or trying to get out of leaving. It was a sad time for us, and the arrival of a group or replacements from the basic training detachment on the field didn't do much to relieve the gloom.

Meanwhile rumors that the 12th was scheduled to leave for the wars flew high and wide. Ground personnel were busy making boxes and packing supplies. There were daily calisthenics and weekly reviews. The words "Pass In Review" became our watchwords, and still thought about with horror. We became good soldiers rapidly and received a commendation on our excellent display from Col. Boren, the Commanding Officer of the First Transport Command, after he inspected the Group. We were fairly certain by that time that we didn't have much longer to stay in the United States. We became even more certain when ten C-47's arrived and were assigned to the Squadron, bringing our number of ships up to the T.O. Requirements. The Pilots and co-pilots of the ships soon made themselves at home in the Squadron, and we all waited expectantly for the next move.

Rumors became fact when Captain Clark with ninety-two enlisted men left for Fort Dix, New Jersey by motor convoy. The ride from Westover to Fort Dix was a long and uncomfortable one, but we knew that we would have to endure far greater hardships later. For the drivers it was a wonderful day. They careened down the roads at breakneck speed and laughed at the patrolmen who only a week before had been their nemesis. Opinions about our eventual destination varied, but England was by far the most popular guess. Australia was considered, but the fact that we were at Fort Dix, on the eastern coast, made that guess seem unlikely.

Back at Westover, the combat crews began an extensive training program. There were journeys to Fort Bragg and Bolling Field. The planes were on the ground only long enough for the necessary maintenance to be performed. But our real work began when we said good-bye to Westover and headed for Presque Isle, Maine. From there we hauled freight to Labrador, Greenland and Iceland for seventeen days. Those flights provided valuable experience for the task that was soon to confront us – the lack of flying across the Atlantic Ocean in C-47's. To Captain Clarence J. Galligan, who was then operations officer of the 12th and then became a Colonel commanding the 60th Troop Carrier Group, went the honor and responsibility of leading the first flight across the pond. He did his job well and brought his flight across safely without incident.

Meanwhile, on the 4th of June, the ground echelon set sail, and embarked on the then perilous trip across the Atlantic.

The large troop ship on which we made the journey sailed without escort, depending on her speed to elude submarines, and it was during that trip that we learned the real meaning of "sweating it out".

AND NOW – ENGLAND

One June 10th, after five days at sea, we came in sight of the shores of Scotland, and that rugged, mountainous country was a welcome sight to our sea weary eyes. The great steamer pointed her bow up the River Clyde, and as she crawled slowly between the mountains, we lost the feelings of awe at her immensity, which we had acquired upon getting aboard, and which had increased with every day we spent exploring her. For now she seemed like nothing bigger than a water bug on that great river between those towering hills. Dusk was falling as we approached the town of Gurich where we were to disembark, and we lined the rails of the great ship, gazing in wonder at this new and strange land in which we found ourselves. The mountains rose straight up from the water on both sides of us, and the lights of the two small towns on either side of the river were like tiny jewels sparkling bravely against the somber background of the darkening mountains. War seemed far away in that peaceful setting.

War seemed a little closer when on the following day we shouldered our packs, barracks bags, and guns and went ashore. Our welcome was quiet, but it was sincere, and should have given us a good hint about the character of the people with whom we were destined to live for six months. Refreshments were served to us on the dock, and we were immediately faced with the problem of speaking English as the Scots speak it, for everyone around us was anxious to ask how we liked their country. We were hustled aboard a train quickly, and there too we found ourselves up against something we had never seen before. The small English locomotive, and the tiny cars with their individual compartments, brought out our first superior smiles. The "Toonerville Trolley", which was our name for the train we were herded into, pulled out late in the afternoon. As we passed through the outskirts of Glasgow we saw the bomb torn buildings and thick ring of barrage balloons, and the realization that war was very near, was brought home to us more forcibly than ever.

That trip seemed interminable, for we rode all that night and until noon the next day. We were still happier when upon reaching the airdrome we were assigned to barracks immediately, and were able to go about the business of making ourselves comfortable.

We ate at a British mess hall during the first part of our stay at Chelveston, but we found it all but impossible to get ourselves accustomed to their chow. The Y.M.C.A. in the nearby town of Rushden quickly became the favorite eating place of the Yanks. Tea at ten-thirty in the morning and three-thirty in the afternoon was one English custom that we thoroughly enjoyed. Not being tea drinkers, we found it hard at first to ease our conscience's when the British trucks came to pick us up from wherever we happened to be working to take us into the N.A.A.F.I. (Navy, Army and Air Force Institute, the British equivalent of our P.X.) for tea. So we developed a taste for tea, and had no more trouble with our consciences. Later on it was discovered that between the British teas and our own American chow times, very little work was being done, and drastic action was taken to curb our newly awakened taste for tea. Another British beverage which was called bitters, and for which we had more choice names, gradually assumed a place in our affections. We were told that it was beer, and although we didn't dispute that contention openly, we never believed it. We developed our taste for "mild and bitters" (light and dark beer) during the many nights we spent in the nearby towns and cities, dancing, drinking, and making friends with the British people.

The England we invaded was rural, dainty and charming. Thatched roofed cottages blended neatly into this setting, creating an atmosphere of untrammeled loveliness. There existed an air of dignified hospitality that we at home commonly referred to as British conservatism. Yet after a short acquaintance these people proved to be real, honest, charming, and entertaining. It was refreshing to get away from the high-pressure type of individual, the American, and really relax. We saw it all through homesick eyes at first, and our restlessness made it impossible perhaps for some of us to find any peace and comfort in this strange country. With the passage of time and after our experiences in other foreign lands, we came to feel a deep and heartfelt appreciation of the hospitality, warmth of character, and honesty of the English people.

Our first few weeks at Chelveston airdrome were largely devoted to play, but with the arrival of the air echelon on the 27th of July, there was plenty of work to be done. The day when the entire Squadron was together once more was a gala one, and for weeks the two different echelons entertained each other with accounts of their travels. The air echelon had departed from Presque Isle, Maine, on June 27th, and had flown the northern air route through weather that had even grounded the sea gulls. They told of mosquitoes in Labrador, blue icebergs under the midnight sun, passes in Iceland, and the strange people they met. Their tales made those who had not crossed by air very jealous. They were the first C-47's to ever make the trip, and they were very proud of their achievement.

The business of cementing the outfit into one solid whole as before got underway with the arrival of the air echelon, and was swiftly accomplished. Captain Richard A. Davis had become our Commanding Officer, and he was largely responsible for reforming the outfit so quickly. This was not the only change we experienced in those first days in England. Soon after the arrival of the air echelon we learned that our name had been changed to the 12th Troop Carrier Squadron.

These changes were easily taken in stride, but one thing we did have difficulty in getting accustomed to, were the frequent air raids. The enemy seemed to have developed an intense curiosity about us and he sent reconnaissance planes over our field regularly. Bombers were sent at night too. Just as we were getting used to their pressure, and had begun to stay in bed ignoring them, they dropped a couple of heavy ones fairly close to us and we were in our shelters in less time than it takes to tell about it. Even then we hadn't learned our lesson well. We were caught standing outside our shelters watching the fireworks and a Jerry bomber came overhead at about fifty feet with its tail gun spitting bullets at us. It didn't take us long to get back into our shelters, and we stayed in them until the "all-clear" was sounded.

We had another fiasco with the Jerry on the day when we were moving by air from Chelveston to a new base. It was a dull, dreary day, and there was some doubt as to whether the planes would take off or not. The first flight got away in good shape, however, and was well on its way when the second flight became air-borne. They weren't in the air more than a few minutes when an M.E. 110 appeared in their midst and C-47's started setting down all over that field. The enemy didn't have much of a chance to make any kills at our expense, for a British Spitfire Squadron that was based fairly close to us sent up four fighters and they made short work of the M.E. 110. A few minutes later the first flight, which had been unable to get through to our new base, returned to the field and landed. We considered ourselves very lucky to have come through that day without suffering any casualties.

The movement to Aldermaston airdrome was completed by the 7th of August, and we went about the job of getting set up in a new location under a new Squadron Commander, Major Jesse A. Tobler. Our new Commanding Officer walked into a difficult job. During the months we stayed at Aldermaston we underwent a strenuous training program. To Major

Tobler fell the job of working our Squadron into the efficient organization that later participated in a paratroop flight that was to become a noteworthy part of air-history. Because it was known that our stay in England was to be a short one, and that it would be a long time before we would again be in a civilized country, every effort possible was made to insure that the men had ample time off.

At Aldermaston we were located within a few miles of the large city of Reading, and it rapidly became the Mecca for all who yearned for the life and excitement of a city. Dancing at the Olympia Ballroom was one of the most popular ways of passing an evening, and many promising romances were born there. We found the English girls to be excellent dancers, and it wasn't long before they were cavorting around the floor in the approved American fashion, and obviously enjoying us. The American boys became so popular with the English girls that a great many international incidents might have occurred had it not been for the restraint and inborn hospitality of the British boys. Good times weren't confined to Reading, however. We were located close to London, and whenever possible we made the trip to that city. We were disappointed at first, for we saw no tall buildings such as we had come to associate with big cities, but our disappointment soon turned to wonder and appreciation. The manifold evidences of severe punishment which we saw everywhere, despite the frenzied efforts of the people to restore their city to its former condition impressed us deeply with the qualities of courage and endurance which characterized the English people. We found the calm mellowness and wisdom of age in London, and we couldn't help but feel that here was a large city that would go on despite the most terrible efforts of an enemy to exterminate it.

At night the city was as black as the inside of a stove, and we were helpless. The Londoners, we learned, have uncanny eyesight, and we often had to let them lead us around like blind men in order to get back to our lodgings. If the city appeared dead in its nightly cloak of protective blackness, it was an impression that was quickly dispelled. The heart of London beats strongly behind closed doors and drawn blackout curtains, and we found it to be a gay city teeming with life, music and laughter, willing and anxious to bring the American invaders under its age-old spell. Although we found London an up-to-date, modern metropolis, that was not so in many of the other places we visited. Many of us were disappointed, or rather surprised, to note how far short of American development this island really was, especially those of us who were from the big cities of America. We thought of electrification, refrigeration and the numerous everyday luxuries as absolute necessities. A great many things were different here but we overcame them with true American resourcefulness. The abundant life we were familiar with gave way to a system of rigid rationing, for one thing, and we had our first experience with the economic stringencies imposed on an island people by a global war. With the realization born of that experience came a better appreciation of the generosity and hospitality of the many English people who had invited us to their homes, and had shared what little they had with us.

We also had our first experience with women in uniform in England, and we learned to like and respect them. An ATS camp located near our field at Aldermaston became a popular visiting place for our boys, and it was a common sight to see American soldiers and British girls in uniform cycling together along the narrow and tortuous English lanes. We held dances at our base, and these ATS girls made them happy and successful affairs. For English girls in uniform, like all their countrymen, were unstinting in the measure and warmth of their welcome to American soldiers.

To many of us, England had proven itself a most delightful and charming experience and to some the beginning of newfound joys. It wasn't exactly easy to break the news of our impending movement and some tears were shed when that news became known. The fun was over; the real work lay ahead. We feverishly packed our equipment and personal belongings and waited. Rumors flew thick and fast but the most popular and persistent rumor was Africa.

The first ground echelon left England on the 16th of October 1942. Shortly thereafter, on the 7th of November, our air echelon departed from England on the longest nonstop paratroop flight in the history of warfare. A flight that at its successful completion opened the invasion of North Africa and the subsequent victorious march of the Allied troops and might have presaged the rout of Rommel and his panzer divisions.

On the initial landing four of our aircraft were lost due to enemy action and one aircraft was interned in Spanish Morocco after losing its way in bad weather.

Richard D. Harvey

THE 60ᵗʰ TROOP CARRIER GROUP IS NOW IN AFRICA

Many of our ground men will never forget those first days in Africa; the landing at Oran, the sixteen mile hike to La Senia airdrome, and the timely requisitioning of an abandoned but still serviceable French bus which finally carried us to our destination, Tafaraoui. We had never seen such a God-forsaken place. The rains had made a quagmire and in it we pitched our pup tents. We had to throw out an anchor to keep our belongings and ourselves from floating away. Two weeks of slogging around in knee-deep mud, and a steady diet of "C" rations, made us wonder what there was in Africa worth fighting for.

The Arabs at least seemed enthused with our presence, for they swarmed all over the muddy camp examining everything and gathering up morsels of food. The more enterprising traded off eggs, oranges, wine and nuts for bits of clothing or cans of "C" rations. They mastered the English language, which for practical purposes consisted of three words—chocolate, choomgum, cigareeets. Of course, the words "mademoiselle and signorina" later became quite popular—but that's another story!

The funniest character among them was a small Arab, who after acquiring a blue barracks bag, punched two holes in the bottom for his legs, tightened the sash cord about his middle and strutted all over the place like a proud pea-cock. For days this baggy Arab supplied us with our biggest laughs and probably still does to this very day.

The Arabs were shrewd traders and took advantage of us on every occasion, but one G.I. turned the tables. He traded off the manufacturers label from a mattress for a bag of oranges and a live chicken. We never discovered who the tricky G.I. was, nor whether the story was true or not, but we told it and re-told it because it was the only story we ever heard in which an American soldier got the better of an Arab in a trade.

Our move to Relizane, which became our first permanent base in Africa, was pretty much of a relief. The field itself was made up of a dirt runway and a few stone buildings. With the aid of a compass, the runway could usually be located under a sea of muddy water. After a long siege of living in pup tents however, the stone barracks held a great appeal for the men, especially since the rainy season was in full swing. When the rains stopped, hot suns dried out the ground, leaving fine layers of sand and dust to be contended with. All things considered, Relizane did prove to be one of our best stops. The French people were extremely friendly and invited our boys to their homes for dinners and parlor dances. An evening meal generally began at 7:30 P.M. and concluded somewhere around midnight. The French are extremely good cooks and worked miracles with the little food then available. Our social activities were secondary, however, and we were busy from the day we landed in Africa to the day we left. Besides transporting the vitally needed supplies of war to the front and returning with wounded, we participated in a number of paratroop drops, the most memorable being the one that secured the airfield at Youks-les-Bains.

On the 3rd of January 1943, a general alert was sounded to prepare us for a possible assault from German parachutists. It was here that Captain Duggar issued his now historic warning, "Some of us may not be here by morning". We spent the entire night vigilantly patrolling the camp area but our vigil was in vain. What enemy troops did land were quickly herded together by American patrols south of us. Occasional truck convoys of German prisoners would put in at our field for a night's stopover, at which time some of us would have the opportunity of speaking to them. You couldn't beat the German soldier for sheer confidence. Despite their prisoner status they strutted about under guard and bragged with an arrogance that almost invited a sock on the jaw. Of course that was during those early months—they sang a different tune later on.

We were becoming fairly accustomed to life at Relizane. Some of our men were even contemplating marriage when we picked up and moved during the latter part of May 1943, to Thiersville, Algeria. An intensive glider towing and paratroop-dropping program was undertaken. Then on the 21st of June we moved again. This time to a new permanent station, El Djem, Tunisia. Not one of us who was present at the time will ever forget that station, and those who have joined us since have heard enough about it to make it seem a real part of their own experiences. We doubt to this day that any human ever endured such a low and prolonged state of privation and there were times when we suspected that even the poverty-plagued Arabs pitied us. El Djem was situated somewhere between Sousse and Sfax. It's sole claim to fame being the ruins of an old Roman Coliseum that was considered to be the second oldest standing structure in the world. In ancient times great gladiatorial battles were fought there and, as history has it, the vanquished were fed to the lions. The passing centuries seem to have had little effect on the immediate surroundings with the possible exception of an accumulation and gradual decay of human and animal deposits. The stench was unbearable and it was beyond the imagination how the Arab colony living in small, barren, stone huts could tolerate their situation. These were our surroundings. The heat was so terrible that work was curtailed during the afternoons and started up again after the supper hour. Temperatures as high as 135 degrees F. were not uncommon, and a breeze resembled the blast from a red-hot furnace. A cool drink of water was our biggest luxury, but was not easily obtainable. Native earthenware jugs that offered the best protection against the heat were utilized all over camp for water storage purpose.

If ever soldiers griped it was at El Djem, and our camp was by far the biggest gripers' colony in the world. Morale was at its lowest ebb. All departments and personnel were housed in canvas wall and pyramidal tents that offered little protection from the hot sun. The only respite at hand was a plunge in the cool Mediterranean Sea at Mahdia. But that was 17 miles distant over a broken down and dust ridden road, and although the plunge in the cool sea was a delightful thing to contemplate, the ordeal of the ride to and from the beach was more than most of the men cared to endure. Then too we hardly had enough energy to move. We were on a steady diet of "C" rations, and we only ate when we absolutely had to, P.X. rations were slim, and a man who doesn't have enough cigarettes is a hard man to get along with. An outdoor picture show was altogether too infrequent, and there were only two escapes from utter despair. One was conversation—talk of the good old corner drugstore, the local bar, of ice-cream sodas, of cool, foamy glasses of beer, and of nice cool baths. The other was the altogether too infrequent three-day rest camp trips to Algiers and Cairo.

During this period of very unpleasant memories we continued an extensive glider ferrying training program that was to prepare us for more serious work ahead. Talk of invasion was prevalent and suspense mounted by degrees. Finally on the afternoon of the 9th of July 1943, combat crews were summoned and were briefed for the big show. That evening our aircraft joined forces with the other Squadrons in the Group and arranged them for take-off. Gliders, with their precious cargoes of slightly nervous but determined British air-borne troops, were all loaded and everything was ready for the invasion of Europe. Shortly before darkness the go ahead signal was given. The mounting tension suddenly gave way to a siege of activity and amid great clouds of dust that completely engulfed everything on or near the field, flights of three planes towing, quivering gliders soared majestically into the skies. They climbed and circled until formations were established, and then they droned out towards the sea.

The invasion of Sicily had begun. Months of strenuous training and planning were finally coming to fruition. To those of us who remained behind minutes dragged into hours, and hours into ages; nerves were taut; little talking was done. Through our minds there raced a multitude of thoughts while we attempted to probe into the unknown—to discover how the mission would come off. Finally during the early hours of the 10th, after what seemed an eternity, planes began to return. How good it felt to hear those engines droning again. The mission had been a surprise and by all indication a success. All our aircraft returned safely that morning. Congratulatory messages from higher headquarters began to pour in. We were filled with pride in the knowledge that we had actually participated in and accomplished the mission mapped out for us.

Days later, on the afternoon of the 13th, combat crews were again hastily summoned and carefully briefed. We were to go over another job, but this time further inland and more hazardous. That evening, shortly before darkness our planes carrying paratroopers joined forces with others of the Group and pointed their noses towards Sicily. Once again those of us who remained behind took up the long vigil—"sweating them out". Some never returned. A heavy pall of gloom hung over the camp for days as we went about our daily duties, but now we could rest a bit. Perhaps frayed nerves that had known no rest for many weeks could be soothed. There was consolation too in the knowledge that we were soon to abandon this unbelievable hell that was El Djem and move up. El Djem with its bitter memories, privations, and utter hopelessness would soon be left behind forever.

THE 60th TROOP CARRIER GROUP IS NOW IN SICILY

The squadron site at Geta, Sicily, was within a stone's throw of the sea, and the cool breezes which came up at noon time and continued all through the afternoon were very welcome after the heat and dust of El Djem. The location and climate were not the only boon we enjoyed in our first days in Sicily. Fresh meats and vegetables were a welcome change after the steady diet of "C" rations we had endured in Africa. Free P.X. rations were distributed every noontime, and for the first time in months the men could be seen offering each other cigarettes.

However, only three days after we arrived, Master Sergeant James V. Ruoti, Communications Section Chief, and one of the best liked men in the Squadron was killed by a landmine while exploring the beach close to camp. Three men who were with him at the time were unscathed. Fate had chosen just one of the men for death at that time. The funeral services, which were held the next day, were simple but impressive.

Shortly after this catastrophe the Squadron began "sweating out" a combat mission. We were alerted on the 13th of September for a glider-towing mission to Italy. On the night of the 15th, Squadron aircraft were lined up with their gliders ready for take-off, but at the last minute the missions were postponed. The night of the 16th was a repeat of the previous night. Then on the 17th the missions were officially cancelled. The cancellation of the missions provided the opportunity for the opening of the Squadron's first enlisted men's and first officers' clubs on the 18th of September. Both clubs were stocked with cognac, gin, and wine. Both clubs flourished even the enlisted men's, despite the fact that it was blown over a number of times by the heavy storms that hit the area. Steak and hamburger parties were held frequently. Despite the fact that the local meat gave jaw muscles plenty of exercise, the parties were usually enjoyable affairs.

Work in Sicily began on the 20th of September. Through all kinds of weather and on muddy fields that made even taxiing hazardous, our airplanes carried the necessary supplies of war to the battlefronts in Italy, and evacuated wounded on the return trips. This job which brought no glory, but which we did well and faithfully, ranks high on the army's list of all-important services.

When the rains came the Squadron was caught with its pants down. Most of our tents were pitched on the lowland at the base of some hills. The night of the first heavy rain was a memorable one for everyone. All kinds of queer things happened. One or two men lay on their bunks and watched their shoes and boots sail majestically out through the tent flap, and found them at the other end of the camp area the next day. Others watched the water rise to within a half-inch of their cots, cursed it violently daring it to reach them and continued to lay right there. Still others spent the night throwing shoes or whatever else was handy at the field mice that sought the comparative safety of tabletops and beds when their holes began to flood. The following day was spent in trudging wearily through the sea of mud, in which we found ourselves, moving to higher and drier ground.

On the 18th of October, Major Bailey, our Commanding Officer, who had become, during the rains, Admiral Bailey, received his orders to return to the United States, and Captain Edwin F. Titsworth assumed command. Four days later, on the 22nd, Captain Titsworth's ability was demonstrated when the Squadron move to Comiso, Sicily, was completed in the short space of two days. Shortly after our arrival at Comiso, the 60th Troop Carrier Group, of which the 12th T.C. Squadron is a part, opened a rest-camp at Taormina, Sicily, and a group of 12th Squadron men were sent there. The glowing reports they brought back caused a great deal of competition within the Squadron for a place on the next list.

Taormina is a resort town which did a flourishing tourist trade before Italy went to war. Its population went all out in their attempts to amuse the American soldiers, and separate them from the money of which they seemed to have such abundance.

The Hotel Miramare, which had been leased by the 60th Group, was a fine modern hotel, and every possible service was provided. Waiters who learned their art in the old days when they catered to American and European tourists served meals in a beautiful, large dining room. The food was excellent and deliciously prepared by a chef who was little less than an artist. Wine could be had with any meal. In the evening a local orchestra played during the dinner hour. Dances were held twice weekly, and they were as close to being real American dances as it is possible for any dance in a foreign land to be. But, perhaps, best of all were the fine soft beds, made up daily with clean white sheets (by chamber maids). This rest camp was in operation during our entire stay in Sicily and most of our men enjoyed two or three four-day stays there. It served admirably in keeping the level of morale in the Group very high.

The main business of the Squadron during its stay at Comiso was aircrew training. The real work of supply and evacuation was resumed in Gerbini, Sicily, to which base the Squadron moved on the 5th of November 1943. At Gerbini, we witnessed the budding of the first fruits of the rotation plan. Three of our ground men went home. Immediately the rest of us began to figure our chances of following them. A number of our flying crews went home on a plan that made anyone with 800 hours in the air overseas eligible for return to the United States.

We also had good news about the crew of one of the airplanes we had lost in the invasion of Sicily. Lt. Charles Powers, S/Sgt. Don Guthrie, and T/Sgt. Bernell Rees were all reported to be prisoners of war in Germany, leaving only the co-pilot, F/O Carrol J. Courrege, unaccounted for.

It was in Gerbini that we spent Christmas and New Years. Though we were away from home, our clubs had been comfortably furnished and lavishly decorated, and gala parties were held for the celebrations. There was American whiskey, an unusual and unexpected treat, and a local orchestra provided additional entertainment. There was homesickness too, and more than a few prayers were said that these would be the last holidays we would have to spend away from home and loved ones. But, there was still a war to be won.

On the 10th of February our Commanding Officer, Captain Titsworth, was relieved of command of the Squadron, and a few days later he left for England to organize a Troop Carrier Squadron for the impending invasion of Western Europe. Captain Joseph F. Wimsatt was appointed to succeed him.

Later in February one of our airplanes carrying 2 nurses and 15 patients in addition to the crew crashed against the side of a mountain in Sicily, killing all on board. The dead from our Squadron were: 2nd St. Ivey Rees Jr., 2nd Lt. Chair A. Reinsel, Cpl. John H. Arp, Cpl. Nicholas Geekas, and Cpl. Cliff B. Webb Jr. The entire Squadron mourned the loss of these men, for the three enlisted members of the crew had been with the Squadron almost two years, and the pilot and co-pilot, although new members of the Squadron, had already made themselves popular with everyone.

But for the most part, life at Gerbini was monotonous routine, broken only by occasional reports that enemy paratroopers had been dropped in the vicinity. Rain and mud made our last months there no less dreary. We came closest to real action when an organized gang of natives was seen stealing gas from the field. Everyone enjoyed the spectacle of "Blood and Guts" Mullaly, one of our blood thirsty enlisted men, stalking through the vineyards and orange groves, rifle in hand, intent on winging one of the thieves. When the stealing became too serious, an organized trap was set for the culprits, but although they were surprised and caught red handed, they managed to withdraw from the field without suffering a loss in their ranks. Target practice became a "must" in the Squadron's curriculum thereafter.

THE 60ᵗʰ TROOP CARRIER GROUP IS NOW IN BRINDISI,

ITALY

The Squadron had completed the move from Gerbini, Sicily, to Brindisi, Italy, by the 31ˢᵗ of March 1944. We found the Squadron area occupied by a British Bomber Group, flying the four-engine Lancaster bombers, but they moved out within two days of our arrival, and the work of bringing the camp up to our standards was begun. It has always been a point of pride with our Squadron, as well as with the entire 60ᵗʰ Troop Carrier Group, that we improve every camp site we move into, and leave it as a highly desirable, and extremely comfortable place for the troops who follow us to move into. Brindisi was no exception.

Before the Squadron moved from Brindisi, six months later, every building had been repaired and put in good shape, two new barracks had been erected, the ground had been landscaped, two club rooms left ready for a new outfit to take over, plumbing repaired in the two wash houses, and excellent showers installed. A barbershop, a P.X., a mailroom, a grease pit, and a garage were all left in a suitable condition for a new outfit to start using them immediately. Our men worked hard to make the camp as livable as possible, and not one of us could help but be proud of the job that was done.

On the night of April 2ⁿᵈ our real work began, and it continued until the virtual close of the Balkan campaign. Re-supply it was called, and re-supply it was—to the tune of approximately 3,400,000 pounds gross that was landed and dropped in the six months in which we operated over the Balkans. We dropped approximately 300 important military men at strategic places, and evacuated approximately 1600 persons, (escaping airmen, wounded soldiers, civilian men, women and children) from under the noses of the fuming Germans. That one Squadron out of the four comprising the 60th Troop Carrier Group, over a six-month period, accomplished all this is a tribute to the skill and courage of our aircrews, and to the untiring efforts of our ground personnel. This work was done despite the best efforts of the enemy to prevent it, and considering that our aircraft are unarmed, unarmored, and were for the most part unescorted, the accomplishment becomes almost miraculous. Almost every one of the crews who participated in these combat missions had experience with flak, and some of them still wonder that they are alive to tell about it. Enemy fighters attacked a few of our airplanes and only the skill and daring of our pilots prevented the German pilots from chalking up a 'kill' at our expense. The terrain that worked to the advantage of the troops we served worked just the opposite for us. Mountains which often soared hundreds of feet higher than they were supposed to, according to available maps, were a constant bogey-man, especially on dark, moonless nights, and the turbulence they created was a source of discomfort as well as danger to our crew-members. Drops and landings in pockets between mountains, which would have seemed impossible to a Hollywood stunt pilot, were an every night affair for our crews, and we received many expressions of appreciation, as well as astonishment, from those to whom we delivered the goods, for the accuracy and daring with which the necessary materials of war were delivered to them.

But all this was not accomplished without loss. We suffered our first loss in the early part of May, when one of our airplanes failed to return from its mission. No word ever reached us as to how and where the airplane went down and we were always hopeful that the crew escaped. Missing are: 1st Lt. Melville C. Thaillie, pilot, 2nd Lt. William J. Hurley, III, co-pilot, 2nd Lt. Raymond M. Hoffman, navigator, Sgt. Joseph Matick, engineer, Sgt. Charles E. Kavanaugh, assistant Aerial engineer, and Cpl. Ernest S. Butler, radio operator.

Our second operational loss came in September, and it was a sad one indeed, for our tour of combat duty was about at an end. Capt. Paul E. Davison, our Commanding Officer at the time, was the pilot, and according to reports from the target over which he crashed, both of his engines seemed to cut out at the same time, and he was powerless to control the airplane's headlong plunge into a mountainside. Everyone on the aircraft was killed, and a heavy pall of gloom hung over the Squadron for a long time afterward. The dead were: Capt. Paul E. Davison, pilot, 2nd Lt. Joseph C. Volk, co-pilot, Capt. Edward L. Quegan, navigator, Cpl. Theron E. Hoxie, engineer, S/Sgt. Peter Gingeresky, radio operator, one Yugoslav dispatcher, and six American officers who were to be dropped on the field.

We suffered still another loss. One of our airplanes, piloted by 2nd Lt. Sam O. Painter, was caught in a severe thunderhead that tore one wing from the airplane within seconds after the airplane hit it. The dead were: 2nd Lt. Sam O. Painter, pilot, 2nd Lt. Clarence J. Wewerka Jr., co-pilot, Sgt. Hampton L. Houff, engineer, and one passenger. S/Sgt. John F. Fitzgerald, radio operator, and Sgt. Frank E. Gross, a passenger, both were miraculously thrown out of the doomed airplane, and although unconscious when thrown clear, they regained consciousness in time to pull their ripcords and parachute to safety. S/Sgt. Fitzgerald suffered a badly battered face, as well as several internal injuries, but after a few weeks in the hospital he was able to return to us. Sgt. Gross was returned to the United States because of the injuries he sustained.

Death came close to us on one other occasion, but was foiled by as expert a piece of flying as has ever been accomplished. Capt. John S. Bowman was the pilot, and T/Sgt. Donald F. Willing the engineer, when the airplane prepared to take-off on a local hop. The airplane had reached a height of about fifty feet when one of the engines went dead leaving Capt. Bowman in the unenviable position of having an aircraft under him which had to be set down with no place to set it down. The aircraft, not having enough flying speed to proceed on one engine, veered off and headed for our engineering area where all of our ground men were busily at work. Capt. Bowman managed to keep it in the air while he performed impossible maneuvers in order to miss the engineering area, pass between two parked airplanes, miss a high tension wire pole and finally set it down in a field hardly any bigger than the aircraft itself. No one expected to see Capt. Bowman and Sgt. Willing walk out of the airplane that was damaged beyond repair, and many a prayer of thanksgiving was uttered when they did. Capt. Bowman, who had had an engine cut out on him while 800 miles from base and over enemy territory just a few days previous to this accident seemed little perturbed by his two narrow escapes. When a few nights later he was attacked by an enemy fighter and had his tail section punctured in numerous places, he decided that he was stretching it a bit too far. Luckily his orders came through soon afterward, and he went back to the United States to recover from his nerve shattering adventures.

Despite all these losses, the Squadron considers itself lucky, for under the conditions it seemed likely that we would lose many more. We are proud of the work we accomplished, and we hope that when the final score is computed, the 60th Troop Carrier Group, and indirectly, the 12th Troop Carrier Squadron will receive the credit it so justly deserves for the victorious completion of the Balkan Campaign.

Although we did the most important work of our long career overseas in the months between April 1st, and October 17th, 1944, it wasn't a case of all work and no play. Each squadron was given one day off in every four, and the men in any way that pleased them used those days. Overnight passes were granted, and aircraft made trips to Catania, Sicily and to Rome, both of which cities were immensely popular with our men. Catania was the biggest favorite, for the war having passed it by quite some time previously, it was more like a peace time city than any other that could be visited on a one day pass. Rome enjoyed a great deal of popularity, but only because of its historic sights. The food, drink, and accommodations there were very poor by comparison with what could be had in Catania. Aside from these overnight passes, furloughs were granted to men who wished to visit Cairo or Rome. Three dances were held in the town of Brindisi, and each of them was a great success. Plenty of women attended them, and no one cared much whether they came for the free food and drink, or for the sole pleasure of dancing, just so long as they came. The second anniversary of the original Squadron's departure from the U.S. was celebrated with a dance in Brindisi, and the date was made a memorable one.

Movies were shown at the Group Theater every night, with but few exceptions, and every U.S.O., Red Cross, and Italian stage show that appeared in the vicinity, was corralled by the Group Special Services Department. (These remarks must have been an after thought because they occurred back in Brindisi.) Both the officers and enlisted men had clubs, and both were amply supplied with orange-ade, cognac, rum, cherry brandy, gin, and ice. Beer was a regular weekly feature, and rum and Coco-Cola became a very popular beverage. Numerous parties were held in the clubs, and a band from an Italian Naval Training Station nearby was brought in to provide music.

Our men were provided with every opportunity for relaxation possible. The air crews were better able to stand up under the night in and night out strain of flying over enemy held territory as a result of the efforts put forth in their behalf by the Commanding Officers, Executive Officer, and Adjutant of the Squadron, and the ground personnel were more than efficient in their work of keeping our aircraft flying.

During our six-month tour of combat duty, we had three different Commanding Officers.   Major Wimsatt, who brought the Squadron over from Sicily, was ordered back to the States soon after Capt. Jack B. Goudy, our Operations Officer, was sent home on furlough. Since Capt. Goudy was expected back, he was appointed Commanding Officer, and Capt. Paul E. Davison took temporary command.   Upon the death of Capt. Davison, Capt. Louie G. Martin was appointed temporary Commanding Officer, and when it became known that Capt. Goudy would not be back, he assumed official command.

As our combat work drew to a close, the plan whereby combat-crew-men with 50 missions, and 800 hours in the air are sent home went into effect, a great many of the older men in the Squadron went home. The rotation policy also started functioning after a long lay-off, and a number of our ground personnel went home. At the same time we received plenty of replacements, so the efficiency of the Squadron was not impaired. On October 16th, the Squadron performed its last mission over the Balkans, and prepared to carry on with it's 'in-between' work of transport of men and materials to and from various fighting fronts. Our history is not yet over, we well know, but looking back upon our past record we can't help but be proud, and we are resolved to make our future history as bright and untarnished as our past has been.

From the salt beds of La Senia, through Youks-les-Bains, El Djem, Syracusa, and Catania, from Belgrade to Athens, they met the enemy in his own lair and took his measure. Neither the arms of a desperate enemy nor the moody whims of nature were ever able to force them to deviate from their assigned missions.

For those of you, our Comrades, who have made the supreme sacrifice, we pray for a peaceful slumber. Your Memory shall ever be cherished by us.

To the others of you, who are still pursuing the fleeing enemy, we say "carry on" till the enemy is completely defeated and you have secured for the generations to come a lasting peace and tranquility.

With the exception of a segment at the end of this book, that ends the portion of the *Memoirs* journal. I am very appreciative to all the men who had a hand in putting it together. Thank you!!!

I now return to when I joined the Group in Brindisi, Italy.

Chapter Eight

FINALLY—BRINDISI, ITALY—HOME FOR NOW

I became a part of the 60th Troop Carrier Group in the latter part of June 1944. The 60th Troop Carrier Group had moved to Brindisi, Italy in April 1944 and had begun immediately the re-supply missions to Marshal Tito until the end of October 1944. Since I was involved in the last four months of the Balkan Campaign, I was a participant in some of what I have already touched upon from the *Memoirs* journal, so, should I allude to it—it will be, at least, from a personal perspective. Needless to say, I have been through the *Memoirs* journal so many times, it is just in shambles and I am happy to be able to share it with others. I am sure that those who did such a fantastic job of helping prepare it in Brindisi will appreciate this reflection as well.

Brindisi was our first experience with an airfield on foreign soil so we had nothing to compare to it. The 60th Group always made an effort to improve whatever base they were moved into. This base, obviously, was no different. The barracks (no tents—thank God!) were fine and the food was pretty good. We had a PX and an outdoor theater—not to mention, a barbershop—so what more could we ask?

We noticed a number of wrecked British Lancaster Bombers scattered around the field. They were four engine Bombers, comparable to our B-17 and B-24 bombers. (The B-29 came on a bit later). At one point we were sharing the field with the British but they did move out a short time later. I remember being told, and this isn't very nice, but when our guys were sitting in the theater at night when the Lancasters were coming back from a mission and would make a safe landing, most everyone would stand up and applaud. It was my understanding that the Lancaster Bombers were primarily used for night missions while our B-17s and the B-24s flew both day and night missions.

I have given God a great deal of credit here and there, but He must have been out to lunch again when Brindisi came into being. Southern Italy, in wartime, was poor, poor, poor and Brindisi was no exception. At least now, we found out what every one of us had conjectured about for those forty-five days on the water.

We were now and for the remainder of the war, assigned to the 60th Troop Carrier Group. We would be flying C-47s and I doubt that any of us had ever been in one unless they had flown in a DC-3 in the airlines. The DC-3 is the same airplane as a C-47 but with different interior, different seating and with paddle propellers for greater lift of heavier loads. Right here is a good place to provide some statistics about the C-47. Then the title, *The C-47 - FLYING WORKHORSE OF WW II*, will prove not only true but also appropriate.

The C-47 was converted for the Air Force from the airlines DC-3, which had been in use since 1936. I understand that over 10,000 had been converted for Air Force use some of which may still be flying in different parts of the world. It has been replaced for the most part by the Air Force with much larger and faster aircraft. When converted, it was designed to carry 28 Paratroops and 6000 pounds of cargo or 18 stretchers with 6000 pounds of cargo. It was stated that its ceiling was over 23,000 feet with a maximum speed of 230 miles per hour. We had no oxygen supply so our maximum altitude was 12 to 14,000 feet and if I remember correctly, our speed was somewhere between 150 and 170 miles per hour. The only thing that is never mentioned in any specifications that I have seen is that it could land in a much smaller field than most (especially any twin engine Aircraft). It had no armor, no guns and was too slow to "out-run" most any other airplane in the war. In the conversion, a large cargo door was installed to allow for large "packs" or equipment to be loaded. The frame and the floor structures were reinforced to handle any heavy weight items that could be loaded through the cargo door. It was a "flying boxcar" and was sometimes referred to as the "Gooney Bird". I don't think that is complementary. I never used the name. I only know that it was the safest twin-engine plane that was ever built; the "safety" features even had "safety" features. In fact, I read somewhere that it has been called "the greatest single airplane ever built". I firmly believe that and I feel privileged to have flown it in the War.

Many of us were assigned to the 12th Squadron. We had other Squadrons in the Group but never seemed to mix. We were greeted almost immediately by the older guys in the outfit (not in age, but in rank and length of service.) They were happy to see some new pilots (even us!!) because some of them had flown their missions and were ready to go home. After we had moved into our barracks and got halfway settled, we started immediately learning about the C-47. Lt. John Hicks, from Fortuna, Missouri, was to be my instructor. We spent a good many hours every day in that

C-47, doing everything that Lt. Hicks knew, and he knew plenty!! He was a good pilot and a fun and decent guy to be around. (He had been awarded the "Distinguished Flying Cross"). I found that most all of the guys were decent and fun to be around, just doing the job they were sent to do and were looking forward to going home. There were a few "hotdogs", but I rather imagine every outfit in the Air Force had some of those. Luckily, I never drew one of them to fly with. The C-47 was an easy plane to fly. Not much different than the UC-78 that we flew in Advanced but obviously a great deal larger and with more power. I can't remember engine size in the UC-78, but the C-47 was equipped with two Pratt and Whitney Twin Wasp R-1830-92 14 cylinder, 1200 horsepower engines. Enough power for short take-offs and it just never seemed to give any trouble. It would fly on one engine, but I almost never had to test it. Also, the C-47 was made mostly with aluminum, except where steel might have been needed for added strength. However, the outside was all covered with aluminum sheeting. I only mention that because we flew some UC-78s over to Hutchinson, Kansas for wing modifications, when I was instructing at Frederick. After seeing that they were made of plywood and unbleached sheeting—I was surely glad when my flying in those came to an end.

On the other hand, the C-47, as I said before, was probably the safest airplane in the Air Force. Finally, after sufficient hours of training in it, we were then assigned to one of the "old-timers" as his co-pilot. I thought it might be a bit soon and was I ready? Regardless there I was a co-pilot. God had His hand in it again, because I was assigned to Lt. William

J. Archibald (Archey) from Long Beach, California. He was about six feet one or two and I, being only five feet five and one-half; we were the "Mutt & Jeff" of the 12th Squadron. I imagine that every new "co-pilot" in the outfit thought his pilot was the best in the outfit but I didn't just think it, I knew I had been assigned to the best. There might have been "hotter pilots" but no better. Archey was a serious, no "hot-dog", no showing off safe, heady, all-business pilot. Here again, my winding up with the 60th Troop Carrier Group and not some Bomber Group, as I envisioned early on, and then to be assigned to Lt. Archibald as his co-pilot was definitely, in my opinion, not accidental.

We "new-guys" had no idea, but soon learned of the Balkan Campaign, which was flying night re-supply missions to Marshal Tito and the Yugoslav Partisans. Most of the missions were "drop" missions. I was never aware of just how these missions all came together. Capt. Robert Weimer, from Youngstown, Ohio, was our S-2 Officer. His department was responsible for working with those on the ground in the various "drop" zones of the Balkan area, helping pull these missions together and make them successful. The planes would be loaded with a number of bundles with attached parachutes. It was always necessary to have a navigator along to locate the drop zone. Once the drop zone was located we would get a Morse code signal from the ground, and we would respond with an established Morse code signal from a light on the belly of the plane. Once that was established, we would fly over the drop zone and the crew would just push these bundles out of the plane. We also had Para-pacs on the belly of the plane and those could be released by switches on the overhead panel above the windshield on the left side. I think there were four Para-pac hangers on the belly of the planes. We never did see what was packed in the Para-pacs or in the bundles within the planes but we were told they all held anything from land mines, ammunition, medicines, food, information leaflets, and just about anything one could imagine. About every third or fourth mission, instead of dropping supplies, we would have to make a landing in a valley. We hauled the customary supplies and occasionally we might have a plane load of VIP's either to work with the Partisans or other important assigned duties. These landings were tricky and fortunately, I never had to make one as a First Pilot. I always flew these missions as Archey's co-pilot. I don't have any idea how many landings Archey had made before I joined up with him but he was a master at those landings. I never knew how many drops he had made along with the landings but he had earned The Distinguished Flying Cross with one Oak Leaf Cluster as well as the Air Medal and four Oak Leaf Clusters. Yes, Archey had earned his right to go home. I never moved over to the left seat as First Pilot until this particular assignment was finished. I have thanked God many times that I was able to fly all of those particular missions with Archey as the First Pilot. Archey and I had some interesting flights together. I remember the very first mission to Yugoslavia that we flew together. We had reached our location in Yugoslavia and as they prepared the "field" for landing, we could see a Partisan running along the ground lighting a row of smudge pots—those were our landing lights and as I recall we were to land on the left side of the "lights". I might add here that there was a German airfield at Sarajevo from which they flew the twin engine JU-88 fighter aircraft. I am sure that was always on everyone's mind when making a landing anywhere near there. Zagreb, in the very Northern part of Yugoslavia, Sarajevo, in the center and Skopje, in the very southern part of Yugoslavia were cities that we were never to fly over because they were all held by the Germans and each had an airfield. When looking at the map, one can see that our "drop-zone" areas pretty well covered the whole mountainous region of Yugoslavia and as I recall, we made drops in Albania and even in Greece.

On this very first mission, after we had made sure that we had found the proper "landing field", and as I saw this fellow running along lighting the smudge pots—I thought, "What in hell are we doing here??" Archey had said to me earlier, "Now when I tell you to hit the switch for the landing lights, switch it on and right off." The pots were lit; we were on the approach and Archey said, "Now!" I did as he said: on and right off. We were right in the top of a tree and Archey obviously quickly pulled up and made the landing okay. That night we brought out a plane load of pregnant women, who had been fighting right beside the men in the trenches. We took them to the big hospital in Bari and when we landed we had pieces of tree limbs caught in the Para-pac racks, some a half inch in diameter. I remember too, on that first mission when the crews that were flying that night met in the Ready-room with Capt. Weimer for instructions, he said, "Now if you get in trouble and have to bail out; if you're caught by the Ustaschies (and I'm not sure of the spelling; they were the Militant Arm of the Serbs), kiss it goodbye or if you're caught by the Serbs or the Croats kiss it goodbye. Only with

81

the Partisans, can you feel safe." I can't remember if anyone asked him how you could tell him or her apart?? On those landing missions, in addition to the pregnant women we had on this load, we also brought out wounded Partisan teenagers who had been wounded in the trenches. I don't think we ever brought out any downed airmen, although many had been brought out at other times. One night when we were bringing out a load of wounded, one man had gangrene and was put on some kind of a stretcher just behind the bulkhead or Pilot's compartment. It was cold and we needed the heat on but if you haven't smelled gangrene I can't properly describe it to you. We hauled them back to the hospital in Bari for treatment and by the time we arrived there the crew was about ready to upchuck. How the man ever came out, we've no idea, but I hope for the best. My heart goes out to those Partisans. We saw men and women, boys and girls who were fighting in the trenches. Hopefully they got paid, but we understood they were fighting just for love of country. As a group, they were very helpful to the American flyers and no doubt to other Allies as well.

I always felt that they would have us land across the cornrows because it would almost shake the instrument panel back in our laps. That really isn't fair because they did the best they could under impossible circumstances. Yugoslavia is three-quarters mountains so just finding any place to land at all, in the dark and into the wind, was a major accomplishment and they did it many times. We always had to hit the coast of Yugoslavia at 10,000 feet in order to clear the mountains. Another time on just a drop, we were unable to get the proper signal from the ground for whatever reason and were heading back to Brindisi. I asked Archey to explain to me how to activate the Para-pac releases, which I was not acquainted with. He said, "After you locate the drop-zone, just reach up and hit these switches." Without realizing it, he did hit the switches and released the Para-pacs somewhere in the sea. He felt like a nut and we both had a laugh out of it. I don't know how he handled that at the de-briefing which was necessary after each flight. Nothing was ever said about it so he must have handled it okay.

On another flight, I think we had located the drop zone and had not made the drop, when Archey yelled, "Isn't that a running light?!!" I looked out on his side and saw the red light, which is located on the wing tip. I yelled, "Hell Yes!" and he immediately dropped in a hurry. I didn't know whether it was another of our planes or a Russian plane, for they were also doing the same thing that we were. It obviously wasn't a German plane because there were no shots fired. Anyhow it was too close for comfort and we didn't have a change of clothes in the plane!

I mentioned that the plane that we saw might have been a Russian plane because we would never have known that they were also flying re-supply missions to Marshal Tito had we not read in *The Stars and Stripes Newspaper* about the Russian campaign. It was quite a spread and not one word was written about the 60th Troop Carrier Group and all the flights it had made. I felt privileged to have played a small part, at least, in that campaign, but my heart goes out to the boys like Archey and the rest of the guys who were involved in the campaign. It was dangerous and as stated in the *Memoirs* journal earlier in the book we lost a number of airplanes and some darn good men. They took the brunt of the entire six and a half month campaign. Quite a few of those guys were sent home immediately after that campaign to what further duty, I do not know.

During that campaign and perhaps even before, the 60th was flying air-evac flights nearly every day. Archey and I got in on a number of those. Where the wounded were picked up at that time I do not know, but they were flown to the Bari hospital. Those were not pleasant flights but very necessary. To see those young men as they were being loaded with the bandages everywhere and stubs for arms and legs would break your heart. Those flights, and later flights, after I became a First Pilot, is why I came to respect so highly, the guys who fought the war on the ground in the trenches. We owe them more than I can put into words and they should never be forgotten.

After the Balkan Campaign was over, and before Archey went back to the States, we had a number of flights that you might call "milk runs" one of which was a trip to France. We had stopped in Corsica for something, fuel perhaps. Archey asked me if I wanted to fly it so I stayed in the right seat and took off for France. I had circled what I thought was sufficient to clear a pass that was on our heading, so I started for the pass. Archey said, "You better do another 360" so I did to gain more altitude, and headed for the pass. It looked like we were okay but the closer we got was somewhat frightening. I had full power and full propellers and we cleared that pass by only fifty feet or so. You just can't beat experience! Had it not been for Archey (and experience) we might still be lying on the bottom of that pass in Corsica.

While at Brindisi, we practiced pulling Gliders and one time after the Glider had been cut loose, we were coming back in to land and we had forgotten to release the tow cable and drug the cable across a small field of olive trees. Every time it hit a tree, we could feel it in the airplane. The only thing hurt was our pride and a few trees!

After the Normandy Invasion, an order went out to the airfields for more enlisted men to fill the infantry ranks due to the loss of men in the Invasion. A number of planes from the 12th Squadron were loaded with men to be taken to Omaha Beach. We made a stop in Lyon, France and because of bad weather we were flying low following the Rhone River. One of our planes hit one of the low hills on the side of the river. The pilot had pulled up but a portion of the plane just in front of the tail hit the top of the hill. I never knew if any of the enlisted men were killed but some of them were okay because they helped to get the men out of the plane. The pilot was injured but recovered to fly again but Lt. Agee, from California, the co-pilot and a roommate of mine, was killed. I remember very little concerning the crash but the rest of the planes reached the destination for unloading and we had to stay the night in the plane on an airfield at Cherbourg. As I recall, we were the only plane there that night. It was cold and our sleeping bags on that aluminum floor of the plane were just a bit chilly. We were somewhat concerned because we didn't know just how close the Germans might be. We slept with our .45 automatics, for all the good they would do if needed, as part of a pillow. Very little sleep, but no problems, and we headed for home base the next morning.

While still in Brindisi, we made a Paratroop drop outside of Athens, Greece. We went in a grouping of right echelons. Archey was a Squadron Commander and we were the second echelon in the group. Our drop was okay but I understood that some of the tail-end echelons were very close to the water's edge. We had British Paratroopers and hopefully every one landed okay. There was no opposition from the ground, luckily, or we might have been in trouble. We made the drop at about 800 feet and I always felt that a kid with a slingshot could have hit us. Just kidding! Upon our return from the drop, this story surfaced and made the rounds of the squadrons. Captain Lou Martin, our commanding officer, was in the lead plane and it was told that he got a message from a crewman, Master Sergeant Robert Moore of Alton, Illinois, "We've got a trooper that doesn't want to jump. What should I do?" The response was "Throw his a_ _ out!" Whether that story is true or not, I can't verify but knowing Captain Martin as I did, I believe he could have given that order. The Master Sergeant, Big Moore as we called him was about six one or two and weighed about two-fifty or more and could easily have obeyed that order! We never saw a lone Paratrooper walking around our squadron. We learned later on that "stories" had a way of surfacing and usually with noticeable embellishment. Enough said!

Earlier in the *Memoirs* journal section, I mentioned the close escapes of Capt. Bowman. I think they need to be expanded on just a bit. The night that he lost an engine on take-off, he had made one of those tricky landings in Yugoslavia with a full load of people. After losing one engine, he feathered the propeller and continued to circle over the valley until he had enough altitude to clear the mountains, which necessitated 10,000 feet in most cases. There wasn't much that a C-47 couldn't do, and yes, it could fly on one engine, although it is mighty tricky "piloting" when you lose an engine on take-off. Another time an enemy fighter attacked Capt. Bowman but it didn't mention what he was carrying. I understand that he had a load of gasoline in those five-gallon cans that were used for just about everything in the service. He just had one layer of cans and they must have been loaded in some fashion where they could not shift or come loose. In any case this fighter (perhaps a JU-88) just took one pass at him. The first bullet started above the cans of gas near the door and four or five other bullets went up the fuselage toward the tail assembly. Had the first bullet hit two feet lower it would have pierced the gas cans and that would have been disaster. That airplane was number 51 and they put aluminum patches over the bullet holes. I remember it well as it was the plane I flew from Italy to Belem, Brazil, after the war ended. That's a later story.

Two or three planes were to fly to Athens on an overnight trip. As we neared Athens, we had the radio on and heard some news describing some kind of a political war between an EOM (maybe it was EAM) faction and an ELAS faction. It was a bloody shoot-out and on our way into Athens from the field, we passed the Parliament buildings and on the steps of a very large building were seven or eight wreaths covering pools of blood on the wide expanse of steps. We went on to our hotel rooms and during the night, Frank Horne, who was on the ground floor, heard some gunshots. He went to the window to see what he could see and a little guy with a machine gun was running back and forth from one corner of the hotel to the other and past the window. At each corner he would shoot a burst from the machine gun. As best he could, Frank was carrying on some sort of a conversation with the little guy. About all that Frank was able to understand was that when the war was over, this little guy hoped to go to Chicago and be a gangster. He surely had a good start because he could handle a machine gun!

The next morning we were out walking and sightseeing particularly past the bakeshops drooling over the Baklava that we saw in the windows. It is so good, as are all of the Greek pastries and so full of calories, but who cares? As we were sightseeing, we started to walk up the hill toward the Parthenon. A Greek gentleman, from Trenton, New Jersey, but now stuck in Greece started walking with us. As we approached the Parthenon we heard gunshots and the gentleman stopped us and said that we should not continue, as there were some political factions at war in the area. Prior to that I had picked up a paper Drachma (Greek money) of a 100,000 denomination. I really thought I had found something but the gentleman from Trenton told me if I found five more just like it I could get a shoeshine. Their money was worth almost nothing.

This isn't very appetizing but it was funny so I'm going to share it. One afternoon when we had no assignments, we were just passing the time of day out near the road that went past our barracks. We noticed this fellow walking on the road. He was in cut-off jeans or overalls, and his bare legs looked like he had been in a fire but we found out he was a grape-stomper in a winery in Brindisi. Sometime later, and the only time that I went to Brindisi, we passed by this winery, and parked at one of the doorways was one of these two wheeled carts that they somehow loaded five or six large wooden barrels onto and had it pulled by two horses. Where they were parked, it was all muddy caused by the horses doing what they have to do when they have to do it. These stompers would walk bare-footed through this muddy mess and go in and stomp grapes!! I've never been a wine drinker but if I had been it would have ended right there. I've often wondered if that is the way they create the various tastes in wine?

Another time when we had no flights, Lou Martin, our Commanding Officer, led six or seven planes out seeing the countryside one day. We flew over Anzio, which is very flat from the sea to the beginning of the mountains and is a distance of about four miles. There had been a heavy rain a day or two before and all the shell holes were full of water. We were flying very low and these water filled holes gave us a good view of what a major battle that must have been. There were wrecked tanks and wrecked airplanes all over the place. In most of the flat land, I believe you could have laid down on your back, stretched out your arms and legs and touched four different holes filled with water. The Germans had been so entrenched in the mountains that the Allies who landed in early 1944 suffered many severe counterattacks and were finally victorious but with heavy losses. I have read a great deal about it and it must have been one of the fiercest battles of the war.

We also got a great view of the rubble that was once Monte Cassino. I had seen many pictures of it before, but after the Allies dropped 400 tons of bombs on it on February 13th the only thing left of it was one wall perhaps forty feet high and fifty feet wide with a few smaller pieces perhaps ten feet high. It was quite a structure but 400 tons of bombs should have obliterated the whole of Italy!

That same day we were up near Rome just looking over the countryside. We were flying in a very loose echelon formation to the right. Capt. Martin was leading the formation and he came to a church steeple and without thinking, just lifted his left wing tip over the steeple. Those of you who know about formation flying can see what would happen to an echelon right! Thank God it was a loose formation because everyone reacted quickly, did what they had to do and no one got hurt - - but it was scary!

Some of our guys got to go to Cannes, France to rest camp and some of the others, including me, went to Rome. Rome is truly a beautiful city with so much religious history. It was the one place in all that we saw; I would like to have taken my wife to see it after the war. I remember when we were there and went to the Officers Club, a young lady who was working noticed the wings on my uniform and let me know real quick what she thought of the bombings of Rome by the Americans. In reality I saw very little destruction. Rome was declared an open city and as a result had been left virtually unscathed.

I remembered so much about Rome from my Latin class in high school that I use to think that my teacher, Miss Virtue, had been in Rome when it burned while Nero was playing the fiddle! We had the time and we did get to see a lot of Rome. We walked in the Forum and the Coliseum (where the early Christians were fed to the lions). We walked on the Appian Way, visited St. Peter's, St. Paul's and St. John's churches. Each one has its own unique points of interest to see but St. Peter's stands alone in that regard. Perhaps the most memorable was the high, high dome that was designed by Michelangelo, though he never lived to see its completion. The other visual that has stayed in my mind over these many years was the forty-inch or so, band of gold leaf all around the interior of the church at the very top of the wall against the ceiling. On it as I recall, was impressive large black lettering of what I believe were Bible verses.

We also visited the famous Catacombs. It was certainly different and I'm glad I saw it although it would be at the bottom of my list of things to see in Rome. The many, many beautiful fountains were more impressive.

Any soldier who spent any time in Rome would certainly remember a nightclub called "Broadway Bills". I was there only once but it was an experience. It did remind you a bit of the States. They tried to emulate the American music not too successfully though! It was so crowded you almost couldn't breathe but it was better than nothing. From what I saw that one night I concluded it was surely a hangout for the Americans. Speaking of Americans I remember someone telling me about the Englishman who was asked what he thought of the Americans and his response was "There are three things wrong with the American service man: He's over-paid, he's over-sexed, and he's over here!!"

While in Brindisi Archey got a promotion to Captain Archebald (it couldn't have happened to a better guy), and was sent back to the States soon after. I heard from him once and he was flying the four engine Constellation out of San Diego, I think. Soon thereafter I moved over to the left seat as First Pilot. I should remember that date but, as important as it was to me, the old mind has just forgotten. I can't even remember exactly when I got my promotion to 1st. Lieutenant. Oh, how I wish now that I would have kept some sort of a log of all the flights. It would have made this a great deal easier. To depend on one's mind after fifty-eight years makes it sort of a "hit-and-miss" situation.

Just before the Balkan Campaign came to an end, Archey and I had a "drop" mission in the very Northern part of Yugoslavia. On the way we flew over Trieste, Italy, which was still occupied by the Germans, but we had never been told not to fly over it. We were at ten or eleven thousand feet and five or six searchlights were trying to pick us up. Archey stayed on course and the searchlights were unable to spot us and there was no flak. That was the only time with searchlights that I had experienced. It made us realize what the Bomber Crews went through on probably every bomb run plus they got the flak. Once they were on the "run" to the target and the Bombardier had control of the plane—flak or no flak—it was straight and level flying until the bombs were dropped. Those guys had it rough, rough, rough and deserve all the credit and respect of every American, even the protesters who don't have a clue that they live in the greatest country in the world! If I were president, I would have each one drafted, given only a slingshot and send them to Iraq to look for terrorists!!

On one flight to Lyon, France, it was necessary to stay overnight and we went to a nightclub where there was a five or six-piece band playing and singing in French, "Flat Foot Floogie!" Some of you old-timers still remember that awful "song" or better I should say piece because song it ain't! I had forgotten that God-awful piece until today when I heard some "music" (my wife washed my mouth out with soap!) and I think they were Emmy winners!

I think (and who cares what I think) the word Emmy should be changed to "crummy" or maybe even "crappy" winners. Such language! There isn't enough soap to wash out the mouths of some of the present-day "singers". Oops! I mean mouthers because singers they ain't!! I'm really showing my age. I'll bet some of the really good singers of all time like Frank Sinatra, Bing Crosby and many others are probably spinning in their graves. My over-the-hill generation was so very fortunate, and privileged to listen to and to dance to the likes of Glenn Miller, Harry James, The Dorsey Brothers, Ted Weems and even Lawrence Welk. How very fortunate we were.

We moved from Brindisi up the boot to Pamigliano, Italy, a bit south of Naples and right at the base of Mt. Vesuvius. In fact we could walk up on Vesuvius from our barracks and we tried it once and about half the way up we were fogged out

93

and never tried it again. Our barracks in Pamigliano were probably the best we ever had. The Germans used them until they were run out of Italy then they were taken over by a B-25 Bomb Group. In 1944 when Vesuvius blew its top another time, the lava ran down on the field and, as we were told, ruined one B-25. Where the B-25 Bomb Group moved to I do not know but those barracks made a nice place for the 60th. I think we might have moved there sometime in early November. I remember snow there one time but a very light dusting. It was chilly though and I remember the women who lived nearby coming over and rummaging through our garbage cans that were used by our kitchen staff, looking for most anything, particularly potato peelings that they could make soup out of. The women were dressed in gunnysack skirts and those wooden klacks, at least that is what I called them, with no socks or stockings, wading around in that light snow searching for something to eat. Yes, wartime is hell on everyone and when you're already poor it makes you even poorer.

With the Balkan Campaign taken care of, the remainder of the war was spent in VIP flights, air evacuation flights, and just plain run-of-the mill type flights. We seemed to always have something to do.

Some flights still stand out in my mind. At Christmas time in 1944, we got an opportunity to fly Christmas presents to some infantry bases in Northern Italy. One stop was at Udine, and what a difference it was from Southern Italy. The people seemed different, the countryside was different, and it looked like a farm community where there was no indication of poverty as was evident in Southern Italy.

Another assignment came along that I really enjoyed. We flew a load of B-17 tires up to a Bomb Group in Burtonwood, England. Lt. M.M. Mortensen from Houston, Texas was the pilot and Lt. Pavloglou from Springfield, Massachusetts and I were allowed to sign on as dual co-pilots, just to get to go on the trip. We landed in Plymouth, England, probably to take on fuel. The wind was so strong and I was flying co-pilot at the time - it is normal to land the C-47 with about half-flaps, but "Big Mort", as he was sometimes called, was so busy man-handling the airplane, he hollered at me after he had already landed the plane, "Flaps up!" He had forgotten to ask for them down! It was a tough landing but everything worked out well so we fueled up and headed for Burtonwood. Plymouth, as I recall was in the very southern part of England on the English Channel. From what we were told, the wind must blow like that all the time. Burtonwood must have been close to London because we landed in London, and stayed over night. As we approached London we received clearance for landing. Mort was only a hundred feet of so from touchdown when someone in the tower must have goofed because a P-47 Fighter Plane dropped down right in front of our nose and landed in front of us. It's a good thing that we had a change of clothes with us. Like they say, "A miss is as good as a mile!" I can't argue that point!

We were hauled into London from the field in an English Weapons Carrier and the first sign that I saw on the side of the road was "Exide Batteries". It was like coming home!!

London had really been hit, night after night by the German V-2 Rockets. We heard nothing that night nor were we able to see the destruction because it was night and dark as pitch, no lights but places were open, though blacked out. We found an English Pub, perhaps to have some of their warm beer and just to see how the Londoners were handling the German bombings and the war in general. They were a brave and stalwart people in spite of the hell that they went through, this Pub, at least, was absolutely packed with people and they were having fun. Gad! How nice it was to be able to talk to people in English and to hear English in return although some of their "English" was difficult to understand, but it was still like being home.

After we left London we flew to Orly Field in Paris. While we were taxiing to a parking place at Orly, Mort taxied behind a B-17 that was stuck in the mud. The pilot had all four engines going full-blast to try to get out and when that blast hit our tail assembly it pulled the wheel out of Mort's hands and hit the instrumental panel with such force that it broke the turn-and-bank indicator on the panel. We had to stay on the field for three days to get the panel repaired. It did give us an opportunity to see a bit of Paris. We got a ride in from Orly to downtown and spent some time just sightseeing. I remember that one of the ladies stores that we walked by had an interesting hat in the window. I knew that my wife could never and would never wear it, but as ridiculous as it looked, I thought it would be a good memento from Paris, so I went in and priced it. It was a light blue felt with about a five-inch brim and on this brim sat two stuffed life-sized doves; one blue to match the hat and the other was white.

Not only were they life-sized but also they were very life-like! In fact they were so life-like that I watched closely through the window for them to move but they didn't. The storeowner speaking in French and I in my Iowa English discussed the price and somehow we came to the conclusion, in American money, it was just over $3000.00. I thought before I went in that if I could get it for ten or fifteen dollars it would be a great conversation piece to have when we got back to living in a house in Iowa. I nearly had a heart attack when the storeowner told me the price and I never looked for anything else to buy after that incident.

I don't remember where we ate that night, or if we ate, but we did stay to see the Folies Bergere that I had heard about. The costumes were beautiful, but extravagant. I bought a small book of the Folies and sent it home to my wife and mentioned what beautiful costumes we had seen. What I didn't realize, because I evidently didn't look closely at the book, was about half of the pictures were of topless dancers. I never heard the last of the "beautiful costumes!"

During intermission we went out in the lobby and a Staff Sergeant who was about half loaded, saw the wings on my uniform and backed me up against the wall and let me know in no uncertain terms had his outfit been bombed by our Air Force. Although I'm sure that I never convinced him that I was not the guilty one, I'm also sure that those things did happen, but the show soon started and both of us hurried back to our seats. We didn't want to miss those "beautiful costumes"! During our sightseeing we did walk to the Arc de Triomphe, which is impressive and also to the Eiffel Tower, which is even more impressive. I have read where the Eiffel Tower has an elevator, but I wouldn't have gone up because I'm still afraid of heights. After the show that night, we went back to the field where we had sleeping quarters, and I never left the field again. We finally got the instrument panel fixed and on the third day, we headed back to Pamigliano. We didn't see the stuck B-17 so it must have gotten out of the mud.

If my memory serves me correctly, we weren't as busy at Pamigliano as we had been at Brindisi. As a result, we played a lot of poker on nights that we didn't have a flight somewhere. Early on, my luck was pretty good and I was sending money home pretty regularly but later on, my luck changed and my wife couldn't understand why I wasn't still sending money home. We played pot-luck and when you're playing with Italian Lira, you really can't tell if you're ahead of the game or not but it was fun!

There were a lot of good trips but the guys with the rank usually took those. I did get one good trip to Cairo, Egypt. We flew some Royal Air Force personnel down there; why we got the assignment I'll never know but it was a nice trip. We stayed the night at an English Installation. I remember the next morning looking out of one of the windows and saw some Pyramids. I know the Great Pyramids are there but whether these were the Great Pyramids, I do not know. We never had the time to explore them. We got to Cairo after dark and not knowing one thing about the airport, I was making a normal landing. I had the runway lights in sight and all of a sudden they just disappeared. I automatically pulled up and they re-appeared and we made the landing okay. I never had a chance to see if there was a hill or some obstruction at the end of the runway but it was a bit scary.

We went into Cairo that night but didn't get to see very much. It was dark and the streets were crowded and quite frankly, I was just a bit uneasy walking in those crowded streets. I was happy to get back to our quarters for the night and get an early take-off the next morning.

One assignment we got was to fly something up to Marseille, France. I remember that the weather was really socked in and since we never had oxygen in the airplane, we decided to stay under it. I think there were two planes and the lead plane may have had a navigator, but I didn't so I was trying to stay as close to the other plane as possible but the weather made it impossible. I'm sure other pilots have had this experience but it was a first for me. Sometimes it was necessary to get so low to the water that I could track the other plane by the slicks he was making on top of the waves from his propellers. I never even thought of the possibility of maybe hitting a ship. I think it was on this same trip that we had to go into Toulouse, France. We stayed the night and I thought when we got there that we could find a French restaurant and get some good French food. We found a restaurant alright but all we got for supper was brown bread and some cheese. I guess that was all they had, after all it was wartime. We left the next morning and the return trip was uneventful. We were so close to Spain it would have been nice to have put in there but there was no good reason to do so.

Not too long after we moved to Pamigliano, the 12ᵗʰ Squadron got an assignment to move a B-25 base from Corsica to Fano on the Adriatic side of Italy. As I recall we were only able to make one trip apiece in a day because of the loading and unloading time. The weather was bad that day as well. Bad weather and mountains created a lot of trouble flying in Italy. As I recall my plane was loaded and ready to go sometime in mid-morning. I'm not sure where we hit the coast of Italy, but we had to fly across Italy to reach Fano. As I said the weather was bad so I found a railroad track that was headed in the direction that we needed to go; I got down and followed the "Iron Beam" to Siena in central Italy. We raised up a bit to get over Siena, but on the other side, I don't remember the railroad tracks reappearing, nor do I remember the weather but I do know that we got to Fano, and even in time to get unloaded.

It was necessary now to find a pass farther down the boot to get across Italy once again to get "home" to Pamigliano. Some of the other planes never got unloaded, and one crew wanted to get back to our own barracks and own beds so they jumped aboard our plane. Down the boot a ways, I saw a pass that looked pretty good and we started to fly up the valley. Not too far in, the ceiling was coming down, the valley floor was coming up and sides seemed to be closing in. I've never been one to trust in anything I can't feel or touch so I did a real tight 180, went back where we had come in and then went down the boot looking for another valley to get across. Fortunately we found a valley and got to home base without any further trouble. The next time I was up in that area, I flew back up that first valley. It was a clear day and visibility seemed forever and as we progressed a bit farther up that valley, sure enough there was a mountain peak about 8000 feet high. I made the decision the first time to turn back, and I hadn't prayed to God to give us a hand but in telling this story to others there has always been someone who asks, "How do you know God wasn't directing you?" I never gave it a thought then but in my later years, looking back, maybe this was another time that God had His hand on my shoulder. Who knows?

We made a number of air-evac missions as close to the combat front in Northern Italy as we could land to pick up the wounded and fly them back to Bari to the big hospital for much needed treatment. Our crew would not enter the plane until the patients were loaded. The injured were hung in stretchers up both sides of the plane and as we walked up the aisle, we might stop and talk to some of the patients. What really stayed in my mind were those young men, 19 years of age up to 30, with stumps for legs or arms, usually protected with a wire basket attached to the stump. Some with bandaged heads as well. I think it was that image that just cemented the feeling that I have always had: my heart and prayers goes out to anyone and everyone who fought the war in the trenches. I take nothing away from anyone else in the war, and particularly my Air Force friends, and many of my friends never came back and those who did went through hell on many a flight. When we did come back from a mission of some sort, we had a bed to sleep in, a change of clothes, and decent food, (at least, part of the time). Speaking of the "dog-faces" (and I have never liked that description, even though it is commonly used) the rank that

I came to respect the most was the Master Sergeant. I always felt that here's a guy that earned every promotion!!! Every person, man or woman, who puts on a uniform in any war, in any position, and in any branch of service, has nothing but the greatest respect from this veteran. At the present time with escalating tension in the Middle East I have nothing but contempt toward all of the malcontents around the world who are demonstrating against President George W. Bush and those who have gone to Iraq to become "shields". I thank God I never rubbed elbows with any objectors during World War II!!

Even in wartime pleasant things happen once in a while. One day two friends and I were walking down one of those terribly crowded, garlic-smelling streets in Naples, Italy. We were walking with our heads down because there are many enlisted men and Senior Officers around and really no one is thrilled to have to salute everyone you meet on the street. As we were walking along I heard someone say, "Harvey, you S.O.B.!" I didn't have a clue, but so help me, it was Dick Fleischer, from my hometown, Webster City, Iowa. We had graduated in the same high school class of 1937. He was in the Combat Engineers and was back from the front to a rest camp in Naples. I had him out to our Squadron for dinner one night and earlier that afternoon, I had taken him for a plane ride to see Mt. Vesuvius from above. The crown of the mountain is quite wide and we did a real tight 360 with the wing tip almost inside the crown. We both got a good look at the depth of the hole and fortunately it was a bright, sunny day and we got a view of Mt. Vesuvius that not many have seen. We had a great gabfest and he went back to his job with the Combat Engineers the next day. Fate would have it that we enjoyed many good times in Webster City after the war.

I had been in Northern Italy on another occasion and ran into a Bird Colonel who wanted to hitch a ride back to Naples. On the way, he wanted to see the Leaning Tower of Pisa. It was on the way and I hadn't seen it either so we headed for that direction. It loomed out as it does in any picture that I've seen. I hadn't a clue how tall it was or it's other dimensions but my Encyclopedia tells me it was built in 1174-1350 and rises to a height of 179 feet in eight colonnaded stories. It is 16½ feet off of perpendicular, which is a surprise to me because it didn't look that far off. We flew just a bit above the top of it and did a tight 360. We got a good view, the Colonel was happy and we headed for Naples. As you can see, we never knew from day to day what might happen. We were not regimented in our flying like some might have been. As long as we carried out our assignment, we were free to see many interesting things that we had only read about before.

In April, as the war was winding down, the Squadron got an assignment to haul some gas up to General Alexander who had started his push up the Adriatic side of Italy. The gas was put in five-gallon utility cans, which were used for almost everything and then delivered to a British base as near the front as possible. The British soldiers were unloading my plane at about 10:30 in the morning and all of a sudden all work stopped as they took their aluminum cups off their belts and sat down for tea. Apparently, at that time everyday, the war stops for tea! I wondered, as we just waited for the unloading to begin again, if General Alexander had stopped for tea as well? At a certain tick of the clock, the war started again, we got unloaded and I was able to deliver another load that day. I had heard about the British and their tea but that was a little surprising to me.

On April 12th, 1945, when President Roosevelt died, the 60th Troop Carrier Group was on special assignment in Bari, Italy. We had been briefed and British paratroopers had been assigned to specific planes. We were scheduled for a very early take-off the next morning to deliver these troops to a drop-zone just outside of Bologna, Italy. We had been instructed at the briefing, to turn left as I recall over Lake Como, and get down again at treetop level. Bologna at that time was well fortified by Germans so I do not believe it was there that we dropped the troops.

I remembered the drop that we had made outside of Athens soon after I had joined the Group. I am in no position to second-guess but I felt at the time it was poorly carried out but with no enemies on the ground, we got by without losses. This time, we were to go in on the water, under the radar, in a V of V's. For those who may not know what a V of V's means, hopefully I can make it clear. The V's are turned around in the air with three planes in the lead in a V and a three plane V on each of the leading V's wing tips. Then behind would be a V of V's, and behind that would be another V of V's until all planes would be in formation. When we got to the drop-zone, we were to climb to 800 feet, make the drop, get back on the deck, make the proper turn and head for home. We were to be the second V of V's and all

I could envision was fighting that prop-wash from the plane in front of me as we climbed to the assigned 800 feet, kill the speed and make the drop. Pardon my bringing God into the equation but bad weather moved in, the drop was cancelled and was never scheduled again. We were told afterward at that drop-zone was a German Panzer (tanks) Division. If it was true, at those speeds and the prop-wash, we would have been in a bit of trouble.

That cancelled drop was the last major assignment on our schedule for the remainder of the war. We did whatever we were called upon to do - milk runs mostly. I recall one other assignment that was a bit unusual. I had gotten the call to fly to the Island of Vis, quite a ways off the coast of Yugoslavia. Unless we were hauling something to some place, we had no way of knowing just what we might be going to pick up. After we had landed, the plane was loaded with teen-aged boys and girls, in military uniforms, obviously Yugoslav Partisans. As I recall, everyone had his or her head bandaged. It was my understanding, they had been blinded fighting in the trenches. It was difficult to be sure of their ages, but they were young. I never knew until after the war that the Island of Vis was where Marshal Tito had his headquarters. On our take-off, just after the wheels had cleared the runway, we heard a loud bang. We were concerned because we just never knew whether someone was shooting at you but we had felt nothing, so we headed for Bari to the big hospital. On landing, when the wheels had hit the runway, we knew what the bang was. We had blown the right tire and on landing it almost shook the instrument panel from its mooring. It was impossible to hold the plane on the runway for long; it ran off into some mud and came to a stop. That was an experience I had only once, and once was enough. I thought about those poor young Partisans in the back and what they must have thought.

There were days in Pamigliano that we hadn't anything to do, and many times we would get a weapons carrier or some other vehicle from the motor pool and go into Naples to a show. Usually the one who got the vehicle sat in the front seat with the driver. On this particular day it was my turn to sit in front. One in the group that day was Lt. Willis Whipple from Boise, Idaho. He had become sick while at the show, so we traded places on the return trip to the field. He was diagnosed to have Spinal Meningitis and he died the next day. It was a shock to everyone and those of us who were with him that day were put on heavy doses of a sulfa drug and were not to fly for a certain amount of time but some of us got assignments the next day anyway. Lt. Whipple was a quiet, laid-back, fine individual who was missed by everyone in the Squadron. I often wondered if all infirmaries were like ours: if you hurt inside, it was a sulfa drug and if you hurt outside, it was Calamine lotion. I don't recall any other types of medicine ever used.

One day when we had no assigned task, a group of us went to Pompeii. I had read a lot about it, but really had no idea what to expect. It was an interesting place but must have been the original "Sin City". The stepping stones on corners, as I recall, were very large stones, perhaps four to five feet in length, made in the form of a man's private parts. Needless to say, that was a surprise but no more so than the Red Light

District (if that's what they were called back then). Over the door of each small room was a painting of that particular prostitute's specialty or maybe some other vulgar painting in the sexual world. It was plain to see why it was so important to the Roman "big-wigs"! Now, just maybe God had his hand in that as well. He might have said, "Vesuvius, cover up that mess" and it certainly did. There were some Red Cross ladies in our group and that was a bit embarrassing. It was interesting, but somewhat different than I had envisioned.

I remember another trip that I was scheduled to make during those final days of the war in Europe. The trip was to Tel Aviv, Israel and I was really looking forward to it. However, I never got to make the trip because a Captain bounced me. That's the way it goes, sometimes. I had some nice trips so I can't complain.

While walking the streets of Naples another time I ran into a classmate from 44-A. He had gone to B-24's after graduation in Frederick, and had flown his required missions. He was back in Naples at a rest camp and I had him out to our Squadron that night for supper. He was a Captain and I was still sporting my gold-bar but that's what happened in Heavy Bombardment. I really felt sorry for him because his nerves were shot. He had to hold a glass of water with both hands and even then he could hardly hold it still enough to get a drink. Make no mistake, those guys in the Bomb Groups caught Hell. You take what life dishes out but in retrospect, I was glad that I never got the B-24 that I had asked for.

I mentioned earlier what I thought about the P-38—a beautiful airplane that I thought I would fly. The closest I ever got to one was one time I volunteered to let the British use me to test a new piece of equipment that would assist pilots in making bad weather and instrument landings. After I had taken off, I called the tower to get my instructions. He gave me a heading for Salerno, which is very mountainous, but only 3000 feet or so, as I recall. I was guiding the airplane, but this person in the tower, in reality, was flying it. He would give me a heading to fly, and almost always it was up or down a valley. You can bet that I kept an eye out to see where I was at all times. This system may have been foolproof but it was new to me. He would give me another heading to fly for a short time, and then another and so on for at least a half hour or so. Finally, he said, "Now, if you look under your left wing-tip you'll see your runway." Right on the button. I never had an opportunity to use that piece of equipment outside of this test situation but I would have trusted it anywhere. Whether it is still being used today or if they have a better system, I do not know. After he was through with me, I stayed in the area for a while and ran into two pilots flying P-38's. They put down half-flaps and got on each of my wing tips. I had the throttles with all the power I could get, with all the props I could get and with their half-flaps and probably flying just above stalling speed. We flew a V formation for a while. That's the closest I ever got to a P-38. It is still a beautiful airplane and served America well in the war.

During the war many pictures were printed of various types of aircraft coming back from a bomb run, showing the damage as a result of running into flak, or having been shot up by enemy fighters. On one of my stops in Bari, I had parked the C-47 near where a B-24 was parked. I walked over to it and there was a hole in the top of the fuselage somewhere between the waist gunners and the tail assembly so large that I believe you could have lowered a Jeep right down into the hole! I was able to talk to someone there who seemed to know something about the history of the plane. I was told that a 90-millimeter shell had gone through the bottom of the aircraft and exploded as it went out the top. Neither of the waist gunners was killed but the tail gunner lost his life. That was the only casualty on the plane and under those conditions, the pilot was able to bring it back and to land it! If he didn't get the Distinguished Flying Cross he certainly should have. The tail assembly was enormous with the two vertical stabilizers. I walked over to it, grabbed the assembly with my thumb and two fingers on one hand and moved the whole assembly just a little but it moved. I thought about the song "Coming Home on a Wing and a Prayer". One would almost have to believe that God might have had His hand in that one too.

On May 8th, 1945, I had been on a flight in Northern Italy and when I got back to the Squadron in early evening, everyone was whooping and hollering and throwing articles down on the yard between the buildings. It wasn't difficult to guess why—the war in Europe had come to an end! Later that evening a Sgt. Jackson, a flight crew chief I think, came through the barracks with a very large bottle of Italian Cognac and demanded that everyone take a swig out of the bottle. When it came my turn, guessing what it might taste like, I just stuck my tongue in the bottle, tipped it up for a second and passed it on. I couldn't taste anything for three days! That stuff would kill a skunk! It was a great day in history and everyone certainly had a right to celebrate.

I doubt that most of us got any sleep that night. The next day, some planes from the 12th Squadron were called upon to haul some Jeeps to Klagenfurt, Austria, just a few miles beyond the Yugoslav border. We unloaded the Jeeps and Capt. Martin, our Commanding Officer, who had led the group flight that day, took one of the Jeeps and loaded as many of us as he could and drove around Klagenfurt. Every road coming into Klagenfurt was loaded as far as you could see with German Soldiers coming into relinquish their weapons. Somehow, Capt. Martin got in behind a truck loaded with soldiers with a machine gun mounted on the floor of the truck near the open end. I thought to myself, we know the war is over but what if they don't? We soon got out of that line-up and drove around the town where many Austrians were in the yards as we went by. I guess I didn't expect to see what we did but as we went by, not a welcome hand was raised to us, just scowls as they were saving their welcome for the Germans as they passed by.

In our meandering about Klagenfurt, we came upon a truck about half loaded with side arms. Most of us would like to have taken a German Lugar to bring home, but for some unknown reason, there weren't any to be found. There were many P38's which is a production copy of the Lugar but much easier to field strip than the Lugar. While we were up in the truck scratching around for a special piece, a hand grenade rolled down the pile and I thought this is it for me so I grabbed a P38 and headed for the Jeep. Back in the barracks, I traded the P38 for a .25 caliber pistol with the German Swastika stamped on the barrel. It's a dandy little gun but I have only fired it once. I got an Italian Beretta pistol for a jeweler friend of mine, Ralph Tucker, the same man that gave me credit and allowed me to buy, on time, the wedding rings for my wife and me. When I got home and showed him my .25 caliber handgun, he told me if I ever had to shoot an intruder with that gun it would only make the intruder mad! He gave the Beretta back to me. The little .25 caliber gun had a holster and an extra cartridge clip held in the holster. The holster looked like it had enjoyed a lot of service; scuffed and worn. I was told that it was probably a German Officer's gun. In any case, I sold the Beretta and kept the .25 caliber gun. Maybe Ralph was right; I hope I never have to find out! It is a neat little gun and is my only memento of the war, not that anyone serving would ever need a memento.

The .45 automatic that we were issued in service and always carried on a night mission was a nice gun but we had to give it back at the end of the war. I target-practiced with that gun but couldn't hit a thing. I knew that if I ever had to use it to defend myself all I could do was to throw it at the intruder and then run like hell!

Now, that the war was over in Europe, we continued to make a few milk runs. Anytime we weren't flying, the conversation was always, "What's going to happen to the 60th Troop Carrier Group now?" Rumors were flying around like crazy. The main rumor was that we were going to Burma, that would mean that we would probably fly the "hump" and C-47's without oxygen are not equipped for that. The transport used over there was the C-46; a larger plane and it was equipped with oxygen and the ability to fly higher, which was necessary to get over the "hump". Anyhow, this turned out to be just a rumor.

On May the 25th or the 26th, the Group headed for South America to our new assignment.

Before we move to South America, I want to share the last page in the *Memoirs* journal because I think it worthy of sharing. This is a Unit Citation given to the 60th Troop Carrier Group at the end of the Balkan Campaign.

R E S T R I C T E D

HEADQUARTERS TWELFTH AIR FORCE

APO 650

GENERAL ORDERS)

:   12 NOV. 1944

NUMBER   233)

CITATION OF UNIT

Under the provisions of Circular 333, War Department, 1943, and Circular 89, North African Theater of Operations, 10 July 1944, the 60th Troop Carrier Group is cited for outstanding performance of duty in action against the enemy in the Mediterranean Theater of Operations from 28 March to 15 September 1944.

In March 1944, when Allied Missions, attempting to organize effective fighting forces in Yugoslavia, Greece and Albania, called for an immediate, substantial and steady flow of desperately needed supplies, this vital task was assigned to the 60th Troop Carrier Group. Overcoming almost insurmountable obstacles in accomplishing this important assignment, the 60th Troop Carrier Group distinguished itself through an outstanding performance of duty clearly exceptional in its nature, method, and in its degree of achievement. All missions had to be flown at night in unarmed and unarmored C-47 type aircraft over unfamiliar enemy occupied areas where hostile anti-aircraft fire and night fighters were expected and frequently encountered. Guided night after night by skillful navigators to drop zones pinpointed amidst towering mountains and ridges, alert and proficient crews, flying at dangerously low altitudes, released packages containing apportioned supplies of arms, food and medicine. Displaying unfailing courage and superior flying ability, group pilots skillfully landed on and took off in hours of darkness, often by instruments, from small hastily improvised landing strips hidden in deep valleys and under constant threat of enemy ground action. Making more than 600 such hazardous landings, planes of the 60th Troop Carrier Group unloaded quantities of critically needed supplies too bulky for parachuting, including jeeps and mules, evacuating on the return trip many Allied airmen, wounded Partisans and civilian refugees. From 28 March to 15 September, this group, flying more than 15,000 hours and completing nearly 3,000 missions delivered more than 7,000 tons of weapons, ammunition, clothing, food and medicine, dropped millions of news and propaganda leaflets, and evacuated thousands of military and civilian personnel. Despite weather, terrain, enemy night fighters, anti-aircraft fire, and hostile ground action, which together exacted a toll of ten aircraft destroyed, and thirty-four combat crew members killed or missing, the 60th Troop Carrier Group steadily maintained its re-supply service throughout this period, successfully sustaining highly effective resistance in the Balkan areas. The gallantry, self-sacrifice and outstanding proficiency in combat displayed by the personnel of the 60th Troop Carrier Group

in these operations reflect great credit upon themselves
and the Military Service of the United States.

By command of Major General Cannon:

OFFICIAL:

CHARLES T. MYERS,

s/WILLIAM W. DICK

Brigadier General, USA

t/WILLIAM W. DICK

Chief of Staff

Colonel, AGD,

Adjutant General.

RESTRICTED

This is a real Unit Citation and very much deserved
particularly by the many who performed their duties before
the group that included me. It would be difficult to think of
words that would commend those guys as well as the chosen
words above. I just feel privileged that I played a small part
in it.

Chapter Nine

OUR NEXT ASSIGNMENT—SOUTH AMERICA

We finally got the official word that we were going to South America to fly one leg of five or six legs to bring troops back to the United States from Europe. We knew that one leg would be from Puerto Rico to Miami, the prize leg of all legs and the rumor got out that the 12th Squadron might get that assignment. Well, that rumor also proved to be false - - so goes life!

For this final trip, I drew plane 51, the one with the bullet holes and the patches up the side of the fuselage. It was packed to the roof with stuff and right behind the co-pilot's seat, against the bulkhead and bolted to the floor was one of those green tanks like the farmers used to have when they had oil heat. I don't know how many gallons it held, but we used it for extra fuel while flying over the ocean.

We left Pamigliano and Mt. Vesuvius and for the last time, flew over the Island of Sardinia and on to the coast of Africa. We hit the African coast around 3:00 in the afternoon, and as we flew around the upper northwest side of Africa, we flew over the edge of the Sahara Desert. We were flying very low and ran across a group of twenty or more Bedouins (or at least they were dressed like I thought Bedouins dressed) riding on camels. We were low enough I guess, to scatter those camels every direction and believe me, they can really move when need be. I never thought about that at the time, but if our engines had quit, for whatever reason, right at that time, we all would have been human "shish kebabs" that night for dinner. I have thought about that many times since. It wasn't very smart!

After that possible fiasco we flew down to Dakar, Senegal for a fuel stop and then down to Monrovia, Liberia, into Roberts Field where we spent the night. We had dinner there on the field, a good dinner as I recall, served by Africans dressed in all white suits. I had no idea what language was used or how we might get along with it. The servers were all men and to our surprise they spoke perfect English! We had been in Africa once before while on assignment in Cairo. Most of the people in Cairo spoke English but it was far from understandable.

We had a good night's sleep at Roberts Field and were up early the next morning to get a good start toward South America by way of Ascension Island located in the central part of the Atlantic Ocean, midway between Africa and South America. When you look for Ascension Island on the map, if you can find it, you can only think of looking for a needle in a haystack. We were flying without a navigator, so we had to rely totally on the radio to find Ascension Island. The radio did its job; we landed, took on fuel and headed for Natal, Brazil, which is almost due west of Ascension Island. That was next to the last leg of our flight to Belem, Brazil. It was on my 26th birthday, May 28th, 1945. I'm very poor at remembering dates but that particular day, I'll never forget! We were a half an hour or more from Natal when the oil gauge on the right engine started falling back to zero then it might go back where it belonged, then fall back to zero. Oil pressure on an automobile is important but on an airplane engine it is imperative and quite scary when it is not functioning properly. Nothing, obviously, was below us but water and more water as far as the eye could see. Many things were going through my mind like engine failure and my feathering the propeller to then make it on one engine, depending on our load. The worst scenario going through my head was trying to ditch the plane as we had been taught, but not with that large tank of fuel right behind the co-pilot's seat. Had I been a praying man, I would have been hard at it. We crossed our fingers, our legs and maybe even some eyes. I kept mine on the oil gauge. The engine continued to function as it should, and when we landed in Natal, the whole right side of the airplane was covered with oil. We stayed in Natal for three days while a new engine was flown in and installed. We then flew to Belem, Brazil, which would be our home away from home until December 1945.

Belem is located on the mouth of the Amazon River, right on the Equator. I don't need to describe how hot it was there, but it was HOT! HOT! HOT! Not to mention HOT! I am sure that it was all jungle before it was cut down to make a base. Our barracks were right in the jungle; by the time we got in the airplane for take-off, we were wringing wet from sweat. We obviously never had air conditioning in the barracks but I really can't remember them being too bad at night to sleep in. Our food was excellent, and every morning when we went to breakfast, right in the entry to the dining room was a huge container stacked with the largest bananas that I have ever seen - before or since!

It seemed like we flew some ungodly take-off times around the clock. I never knew where the pick-up point was in Europe or which Squadron picked up the troops. One Squadron brought them from Natal to Belem, and we would take them to Georgetown, British Guiana. Another Squadron would take them to Puerto Rico and then another Squadron would take them to Miami, Florida and then eventually home.

Even before we put in at Belem, we stopped at a field in Trinidad and unloaded all parachutes. I thought this was strange at the time but we found out that the thought was, if you did go down in the jungle, and our entire assignment was over jungle, you had a better chance of survival as a group than you would as a solo parachutist. We did have three inflatable rafts in the plane and we crossed three major rivers, thinking again, that we could ditch in one of the rivers, if we were lucky, and then would float or paddle to the coast and would then be picked up, if we were lucky.

We had three call-in stations on the way that we absolutely had to call in every time or we would be assumed to be down somewhere. The call-in stations were Amapa, Brazil and Cayenne, French Guiana and Zanderij, Dutch Guiana. These call-in stations were along the coast and our entire 800-mile flight was all jungle. After getting a good look at the jungle, I'm sure the decision to dump the chutes, was the right decision. I always felt that as thick as the jungle was, we could pancake that C-47 down in the top of the jungle and live. Getting out of the jungle was another matter. Of all the flights we made, none were lost in the jungle.

We never had to worry about mountains in South America like we had to worry about in Italy and particularly in Yugoslavia. There may be areas with worse weather and thunderheads than we experienced in South America, but I haven't flown in any. Everyday the thunderheads would start developing on the Amazon River around 2:30 P.M. and continue on into the night. Some of them would top out at about 40,000 feet. We flew at assigned altitudes, 8000 feet going to Georgetown and at 9000 feet on the return trip to Belem. In the daytime we could fly around the thunderheads but at night we tried to stay on the proper heading and took whatever came. Some of those had such violent up and down drafts and turbulence that you sometimes wondered if the wings would stay on!

Once on a day flight, my co-pilot was flying the plane heading for Georgetown at the 8000-foot altitude. We hit one of those thunderheads with a violent up-draft and he made no effort to correct and stay at the assigned 8000 feet and when we popped out the other side, we were about a hundred feet or so below an Eastern Airlines C-46 just ready to head into the thunderhead, right on our path. Again, a miss is as good as a mile, but this time we didn't have a change of clothes!

On one night flight, we flew into a terrible thunderstorm with lightning all around us and raining like crazy. We hit one of those thunderheads and the turbulence was so horrendous that we tried to find a lower altitude where the turbulence might not be as bad. We popped out of it at 1400 feet and I don't believe we had any further trouble that night. We normally carried twenty-three troops with their baggage and after the hell that most of them had gone through on the ground they surely didn't need it in the air.

We always had a listing of the names and dog-tag numbers of each planeload of troops. I always looked over the numbers to see if any were from Iowa. One night I recognized a name and it was a guy, John Biggs that I had graduated with from high school in Webster City, Iowa, in 1937. I think he was with the Red Bull Division who had gone up through Italy and caught hell but now, was on his way home, and that was all that mattered! My heart still goes out to those guys who fought the war in the trenches. No one, including me, can even guess the hell that they went through!!

The flight that I remember so well, and perhaps the worst situation that did happen while flying the Green Project, as it was called, was one that I wasn't close to. I only saw the plane afterward and heard the story told a number of times. The pilot was from our 12th Squadron, but the co-pilot was from the 11th Squadron. It was a night flight and not too far out of Belem, they hit a bad thunderhead, with horrendous turbulence that threw the troops around bruising and scraping most of them. After they made it through, they talked it over trying to decide whether or not to turn back and take a chance of hitting another thunderhead. They decided to go on. They hit a second thunderhead and then a third one, neither of which was as bad as the first. Incidentally, the seats on that Military plane were made of rather thin plywood and anchored up each side of the plane, leaving an aisle in between. The hot air duct that went the length of the interior and fastened to the ceiling of the plane was also made of thin plywood. On this infamous flight most of the seats and the hot air duct had been torn loose and trampled on causing the bruises and abrasions on the troops. It was my understanding that it put every man in the hospital none too serious, luckily. After the plane landed, it was pulled over to a junkyard. The wing tips were turned up and the fairing, I believe it's called, around the wing roots where it fastened to the fuselage, was gone. It had been torn off! The co-pilot said that he would not fly that project anymore. In any case, he did take a flight on Eastern Airlines back to Belem.

I have no way to prove the outcome of this story, but some of the other decisions that I had heard about, make me believe that it might just be true. I discovered later that the result of that incident was concluded to be due to pilot error and the officer was transferred to Amapa, one of the call-in stations. I had heard of crazier decisions regarding pilot error but if this one is true, the Board that made that decision should have been court-martialed! They must have all been Ground Officers.

We did have some interesting flights now and then. On one flight I remember, we had arrived at Georgetown early in the morning and I had noticed the many patches of ground fog over the jungle. When we arrived at the field it was socked in. I called the tower and visibility was almost zero. I doubted that I had enough fuel to find another field so I just flew around awhile to see if the fog would dissipate. It didn't. In this part of the world when making landing strips a lengthy path is cut out of the jungle leading up to the end of the runway. On this flight I noticed that the path was not fogged in so I called the tower, advised them what I was going to do and confirmed that there were no planes sitting on the runway. I got clearance to land, lined up in the center of this path and touched down on the runway okay. As I flew past the tower, it was just barely visible! The landing was fine and the troops that I was carrying had no idea what was going on.

On another flight, after the troops and their baggage had been loaded, we were walking to our seats to prepare for take-off, when I noticed that the baggage was in a pile right by the door. I never gave it another thought. I want to explain here for the benefit of those who haven't flown in a C-47; between the pilot and co-pilot's seats is a quadrant that holds the controls for the engines and the propellers. On the C-47 in addition to those controls there is also a wheel that activates a trim-tab that controls the up and down motion thus controlling the level of the flight. It had a red mark on the wheel and normally that red mark is right on top when taking off. On this flight, I had gone through the normal take-off procedure except this time the plane left the ground at about forty miles an hour when normally it was eighty, as I recall. All that baggage piled by the door made the plane tail-heavy. It took all the strength I had with both hands on the wheel to hold the nose down. I couldn't let go with my right hand so I yelled at my co-pilot to hit the trim-tab wheel, which he immediately did and I was then able to hold it level until we had enough flying speed to begin our normal ascent. From then on I was very much aware of how the baggage was loaded and exactly where I thought the trim-tab wheel should be, depending on the load. Experience is a great teacher!

Except for the hot weather, Belem wasn't too bad. There was a lot of poverty there but also some nice areas. There was a restaurant called Madame Garays (this is not how it was spelled, but is how it was pronounced). It took two or three letters written to my wife to convince her that it wasn't a house of ill repute. It was a fine restaurant and we only went there when we got our paychecks. They routinely had a certain kind of chicken, Filet Mignon and homemade ice cream. It was always all-you-can-eat of the filets and the chicken and you can bet that we always took advantage of that!

While in Italy and flying nearly every day or night, I picked up a lot of C-47 time and had visions of going into the airlines when I returned to the States. So, when we got to Belem I told the Operations Officer if any of the older pilots wanted to stay on the ground that I would take their flights and try to get all the time in the air and all the time I could get in the C-47. Whether that had anything to do with it, I don't know but I did get at least a couple of flights a week. I never did see (and I really would like to know) the number of troops that we brought back but it must have been quite a few because we did that for about five and a half or six months. On some of the flights in Italy and in South America, occasionally I would get a Crew Chief on the flights by the name of Stanislaus Boleslaw Zamichinski. He told me once that he was twenty-five years old before he could spell his full name. On every flight we had to register everyone aboard the plane on the Form One. I'm not sure I have spelled his name correctly now, nor do I remember how we put it on the Form One. Had we registered his name in full with the engines running, we might have had to refuel the plane before take-off! I'm sure he got a lot of kidding from his buddies but he was a really intelligent individual.

The rumor had gotten around that we would soon be through with this assignment and needless to say, it soon came to pass and it was good-bye South America, hello North America and home!

It was mid-December, 1945 when the assignment really ended. We packed our belongings and prepared for the trip home. I assume that we had to fly the planes back to the States, landing first in Miami, where we went through a quick check to see if we had brought in anything bad from South America. From there it was to Selfridge Field in Detroit. There, we returned most, if not all of the flying gear that we had been using including my beloved leather flight jacket, which I really wanted to keep, and thought I deserved! From there it was to Wold-Chamberlain Field in Minneapolis-St. Paul for further mustering-out procedures. I had some free time while in Minneapolis-St. Paul and I took advantage of it to check with Northwest Airlines about the possibility of getting a job flying. I was told that I would have to ride the right seat (co-pilot) for three years at $290 a month. In those days the pay was certainly adequate, but I had about 1000 hours in the C-47 and I guess I just wasn't looking forward to riding the right seat for that length of time. I am sure that it was a mistake not to have pursued it further. I have made a number of mistakes in my life however, that was probably the major one. I have a great nephew who has been with Northwest for some time now. He has just been made a First

Officer and will soon be flying the new Airbus 330 – quite an airplane! Maybe I envy him a bit!

Soon after my meeting with Northwest Airlines, I caught the Rock Island Zephyr passenger train headed for Webster City and home! This passenger train doesn't go through Webster City – only freight trains go through there and on a different line.

Although the ride from Minneapolis was not too terribly long, it did give me an opportunity to completely relax and let the old mind wander. No doubt, the first thing on my mind was, "After two and a half years – I'm going home!" In addition to that, my mind couldn't help but go back over that two and a half years, picking out the high spots and the low spots like the change that takes place in ones everyday living; the necessary discipline; all of the calisthenics to get in shape for what was to come; making hurried friendships – some good and some bad; the hated "Class System"; and most of all the end result of that two and a half years! Did my tiny bit help in the overall war effort? Did I feel satisfied with my performance? Was I a better man for having served? The answer to those questions was, yes! I know that I am a better man because I grew a great deal closer to a God that I never really knew before. I was sure that He had His hand on my shoulder a good many times in those two and a half years. I know that I gained a greater appreciation for the good old U. S. of A. than I ever had before. We Americans take many things for granted without realizing that someone before us might have given his or her life in order for us to have the great country that we have!!

I must admit (and I am sure there were many jobs in Service, that one could call rewarding), but as I think back (and I never gave it a thought during the war), most of my entire time in Service was rewarding. Passing all tests and learning to fly was rewarding to me personally, as was teaching others in Twin-Engine. Being an instructor was rewarding and hopefully, was rewarding to my cadets! Even overseas, every flight that I made, either as a Co-pilot or as a First Pilot, was rewarding to someone. While flying the missions to Marshal Tito, we were flying supplies to help the Partisans fight and defeat Hitler; and to bring out the injured to a hospital where they could be taken care of and eventually sent home. I recall the Christmas in 1944 when we flew one or two planeloads of Christmas presents from home to an Infantry Base in Northern Italy. The happy looks on the recipient's faces were rewarding! Our flights in Belem were certainly rewarding to our soldiers because they were on their way home, as well as to us for being able to lend a helping hand. The one flight that comes to mind that was not rewarding to either the GI's or to me was the flight that we flew to Omaha Beach.

On the train trip to Iowa, I was in uniform and I left my service hat in my seat and went to the dining car for lunch. When I came back to my seat, a nice looking young lady (perhaps just a bit heavy!) had taken the seat beside me. She was also in uniform so naturally we began a conversation. She was a nurse from the Minneapolis area and was trying to go through the necessary procedures to be sent overseas. I asked her why she wanted to go overseas and she informed me that she wanted to make some of that "easy money". I knew what she meant and we didn't discuss it any further!

127

She was very friendly and conversation was very easy. I often wondered why she chose that seat because the passenger car was nearly empty. Maybe it was the hat! I don't think I even wished her luck in her desired endeavor nor did I tell her that she might find the competition pretty tough depending on where she might be sent!

Not too long after that encounter, I arrived in Ames, Iowa (thirty miles from Webster City) where I got off the train. My wife, Marge and my son, Ron, were there to meet me. After a year and a half overseas and not seeing family, those are moments that you can't easily describe but you'll never forget. Ron was only three months old when I was called to duty, and now had just had his third birthday on December 6th. His looks had changed considerably from when he was born. (Thank God!) That's a moment that I'll never forget. Marge had kept me supplied with plenty of pictures so I knew that he had become a really cute kid even with that head of curly hair!

Chapter Ten

FINALLY, BACK TO THE STATES, WHAT'S NEXT?

Yes! The "War-To-End-All-Wars" (as it has been described) is now history, although in today's school systems, and those responsible for the textbooks, in ten years or less, may not even mention it! Regardless of that possibility (I can't do anything about that anyhow) it was great to be home again and to get back to a normal life. Anyone in his right mind will admit that war is hell but I think the wives back home went through as much hell as some of the guys in uniform. They had youngsters to raise; telephone calls to sweat out; to try and get by on Service pay (plus what we were able to send home from poker winnings??), etc. I will admit that my time in Service went rather quickly. It was a busy, busy time from the first day in San Antonio to the final flight in Belem, Brazil. There was little time to dwell on yourself and what might be ahead.

I had given a great deal of thought to staying in the Air Corps, because I thoroughly enjoyed all of my time there (except as an under classman). My wife and I discussed it and neither of us was too thrilled about the prospect of always changing schools for Ron and any other children that we planned to have. I've known those who went through that very thing and it all worked out okay for them. Perhaps the main reason for not staying in was that I thought any promotions might be difficult to come by since I didn't have college experience. I can understand this but I might have been wrong too. I have no regrets for the two and a half years in the Service of the greatest country in the world! I learned discipline; I learned respect; and I came out a much better patriot than when I went in. I thought I had learned a bit more patience, but if I had I have lost it in my later years as I now witness the many protesters who march, burn and destroy private property for the flimsiest of causes! Many don't even have a cause and are just being led by a professional agitator who probably can't hold a steady job! What is so disturbing to me is that they get by with it. I would not want to serve with them in battle but if the draft was again imposed, I'm of the opinion they should be the first to be drafted! Army discipline would do them a great deal of good.

So, after returning home, I did stay in the Reserves for awhile, but being back with family, it wasn't too difficult to decide that the Reserves wasn't for me so I resigned - rightly or wrongly. In retrospect, with the current high cost of prescriptions, had I made the Service a career the check that I would now be receiving would certainly come in handy! Isn't hindsight great?!

I was now out of a job for the first time in my life since I started carrying newspapers in the ninth grade. I had received my mustering-out check for $300, which, incidentally, I spent on a Muskrat coat for my wife. She did get a lot of wear out of it so I guess the money was well spent. In those days you could wear a fur coat and not have to worry about some nut spraying you with paint.

I probably could have gone back to work at the drycleaners but I was only making $18 a week when I left and $18 wouldn't have gone very far in 1945! Even before I had time to think about employment, I had to take Ron down to the barbershop and get his curls cut off. Then he at least would look like a boy. I will admit that it nearly caused a divorce (just kidding) and it was a couple of months before my mother-in-law would speak to me!

Unbeknownst to me, and I don't think that my brothers Jess or Delbert, knew about it either, our brother Fred was in business in Estherville, Iowa. He and another brother Jim, who worked at the Dodge Plant in Chicago during the war making B-29 Engines, had gotten their heads together and decided that Galesburg, Illinois needed an electric shop. One that could rewind all sizes of electric motors, take care of automobile starters and generators and later alternators. They felt that it could provide a good living for the five of us – Delbert, Jim, Fred, Jess and myself. Jim had already started the shop in Galesburg, and I really didn't know what I wanted to do, so I agreed to be a part of it. When it was being discussed early on, I was in South America, Delbert was a P-47 mechanic in the Pacific, Jim was in Chicago, Fred was in Estherville, Iowa and Jess was in a government plant in Towson, Maryland. As each one of us could come in with our investment of $1500, we put on our work-aprons and went to work. It turned into a very good business and in fact it is still in Galesburg operated by my three nephews.

Galesburg was a city of about 35,000 at the time we all bought homes. My second son, Doug (and the last) was born in the third house that we owned there and in 1950 we built a nice split-level that we lived in until we left Galesburg. During that period we experienced one of the more enjoyable times

131

of our married life. It was rather hectic sometimes because we had only one car. Ron was playing baseball in the Junior League and Doug was playing in Little League. Ron's play was on the south side and Doug's play was on the east side. To get them to the games, when the starting time was the same and to be able to see parts of both games became rather difficult. It was a great time and Doug went on to play college ball. Ron and Doug both graduated from high school in Galesburg and then went on to college – Ron to Purdue University in Lafayette, Indiana and Doug to Carthage College in Kenosha, Wisconsin. We had talked college to both of the boys as soon as they were old enough to understand English. Both attended the colleges they wanted and graduated with degrees that they had chosen. Both married well and no divorces. Ron has two daughters; his youngest now has four children; three boys and a girl. Doug has a son and a daughter. So, all in all, Galesburg treated us well and we've got a lot for which to be thankful!

Most of my life, in the back of my mind, was the desire to be in the restaurant business. (Don't ask me why!) Although, I am a recipe nut and love to cook. I must have over 300,000 recipes on file. I am in the process of putting together a cookbook – for men only – although I may never get it done. I collected all of those recipes from California to Florida in various doctor's offices before the women got a chance to cut them out.

I think my love for cooking (maybe out of desperation) began when Marge and I were newly married. She had made a sponge cake and it certainly was a sponge. I sold it to a carwash; they used it for about six months then asked us if we could keep them supplied in the future! She wasn't one of those wives who couldn't boil water – she could boil the water but I got tired of it seven days a week! That's not all true, but she doesn't like to cook and I do so it works out well.

To satisfy my desire for the restaurant business, in 1965, my brothers bought my shares of the electric shop and I invested the money in two IHOPs (International House of Pancakes). It was a dog's life and turned out to be a disaster. I still think they make the best pancakes in the business but there were problems.

During my time with the electric shop in Galesburg we bought many parts for the business from different manufacturers, all with different numbering systems. So for our own benefit, I perfected a numbering system just for us - one for the incoming products and a numbering system for our own outgoing products. So after the pancake fiasco, I went to the International Products & Manufacturing Company in Chicago. This was a company we bought a lot of parts from in Galesburg and I had met the owner a time or two. I made an appointment with Mr. Al Mansfield, the owner and informed him that I had perfected a numbering system that he might be interested in. I explained the idea and it must have been an opportune time because his company had used up nearly all of their numbers through 9,999 and were going to experience some sort of a problem in the system when they went into the 10,000's. In any case, after explaining it he informed me that he would only be interested in the idea if I came with it. He offered me a deal and I spent the next nineteen years with IPM. As I grew older, we spent a number of vacations at Fort Myers Beach, Florida and decided that we might want to retire there someday. We liked Cape Coral (across the river from Fort Myers) and learned about a lot that was for sale. With the help of a friend who lived there and advised us to buy it, we did, over the phone. We later built a house, over the phone again because another friend was able to get it rented to a minister and his family even before it was built. I learned that this minister went to check the building progress of that house about everyday. As soon as it was finished he and his wife moved in and lived there for about two and a half years. Ultimately they decided they would like their own home, so I was forced to do something that I hadn't planned on.

I was nearing retirement age and we couldn't afford two places. We were living in a condominium in Palatine, Illinois, very near to where I was working. I wasn't too thrilled about re-renting our house in Cape Coral to just anybody with our being so far away in Illinois. I approached my General Manager who was a good friend and explained the problem. He said to me, "I'm not happy with our salesman down there. How about moving you down there and you handle the sales in Florida?" (Maybe God had His hand on my shoulder again!) Of course I jumped at the chance for that job and worked until 1982. I had reached sixty-two and decided to retire and I haven't been sorry one minute! In fact, I would have retired right out of high school, but I had learned early on that I needed to eat to live and that requires money.

We lived in our house for ten years; played a lot of bridge and golf and loved every minute of it, in spite of the many 90-degree days from April to October. In order to have a nice yard in Florida, it took many hours a week of mowing and each bush or flower had its own particular bug or worm that necessitated a number of different chemicals and hours of spraying! Despite of all the yard work, I found time to play a lot of golf with the guys.

When the yard work got to be too much, we decided to come to Indianapolis to be around the only family we have. We bought a condominium and haven't regretted that either! We have enjoyed our grandkids: Ron's girls were pretty well grown by the time we moved here and later I had a part in each of their marriage ceremonies which I enjoyed very much. We have been able to watch and enjoy Doug's two kids growing up their entire lives. We enjoy our four great-grandchildren, and I marvel at my granddaughter's ability to so easily handle her brood. I remember just the two that Marge and I had and I get goose bumps! Just age I guess. Whoever made the statement, "Children are made only for the young" - sure hit the nail right on the head. I read some place that children are a great comfort in your old age; they help you reach it faster too! No argument there. I don't necessarily agree with Eve Arden who said, "Alligators have the right idea, they eat their young!" Although the saying may very well be true that grandchildren are God's reward to grandparents for not having drowned their own children! (I'm only kidding.)

Chapter Eleven

MEMORIES AND REFLECTIONS OF 85 YEARS

On the 28th of May 2004, I celebrated my eighty-fifth birthday in Washington D.C. My son Ron and I, along with another man and his son who made all of the arrangements, drove into Washington D.C. to be part of the dedication ceremony of the World War II Memorial. I'll touch on this later.

As I look back over these many years, there are only five birthdays that really are memorable: My "0" birthday was the most important because without it there wouldn't have been any others! When I turned eighteen I graduated from high school. On my twenty-sixth I was sweating out an oil problem in the right engine on the C-47 that I was flying from Ascension Island to Natal, Brazil in 1945. My eighty-first was significant because in my younger days I always wanted to see the 2000 calendar (the literal turn of the century) hanging on the wall. When it finally came it didn't mean that much, but I did live to witness it and that was all that mattered. My eighty-fifth is very significant because I made it! It will be the easiest one to remember because I spent it at the World War II Memorial in our nation's capitol. Not to mention, when I got home I was lighting the candles on my birthday cake, when the last one was lit the first one had burned into the cake and gone out! What is really irritating I've discovered, is that I'm too old for castor oil and still too young for Geritol. I never thought that I would ever have to take a nap to get ready for bed at this age. There are a lot of funny stories about old age and we do need to laugh. It was Will Rogers who said, "We are all here for a short spell so get all the good laughs you can." The only thing worse than growing old is to be denied the privilege. Amen.

A lot of water has gone under the bridge (or over the dam) during those years. Whether or not Tom Brokaw is correct about *The Greatest Generation* – a book that I would highly recommend, it has been a great and mind-boggling century in which to live. Who knows, the next century may be even more mind-boggling. We witnessed and lived through the Great Depression. We saw four wars including the "War To End All Wars". Now we are in perhaps the toughest one of all, the war on terrorism. At least in World War II we knew who the enemy was and where he was located. We could kill or capture him on foot or we could obliterate his whole location from the air. The terrorists are coming at us from so many locations, are hard to find, are isolated and are attacking from civilian homes in civilian vehicles. How can anyone discern what is a bomb-laden car and what is a car on its way to work? This eliminates the obliteration tactic. It's a different kind of war and one that's going to be a lot harder to win but must be won at all costs.

Television allowed us to witness the destruction of the World Trade Center in New York City with the loss of nearly 3000 innocent civilians. Who, in any state of mind, could have imagined a man, even a terrorist, committing that kind of act on his fellow man? The picture of that 767 loaded with passengers hitting that second tower is as vivid in by mind as it was on September 11th. We have witnessed on TV thousands of acres of forest being burned due to the carelessness of man. We have witnessed hurricanes, tornadoes, earthquakes, and floods. Thank God man hasn't figured out how to start those! Man gets involved again in the drive-by shootings, the shootings in homes and schools, crimes in the streets and car crashes not to mention the thousands who die from disease. I don't want to be morbid but that's why I so cherish my eighty-fifth birthday!

Since I am reflecting I think it is a good time to share with you a piece that someone sent to me years ago that describes much better than I the many things that have happened in our lifetime. I used this in a writing that I prepared for our fortieth high school reunion back in 1977.

"THE CLASS OF 1937 B.C. (BEFORE COMPUTERS)"

We were before television, Penicillin, polio shots, antibiotics and Frisbees. Before frozen foods, nylon, Dacron, Xerox and Kinsey. We were before radar, fluorescent lights, credit cards and ballpoint pens. For us, time-sharing meant togetherness, not computers. A chip meant a piece of wood, hardware meant hardware, and software wasn't even a word. In our time, closets were for clothes, not for coming out of, and a book about two young women living together in Europe could be called Our Hearts were Young and Gay. In those days, bunnies were small rabbits and rabbits were not Volkswagens. We were before Grandma Moses and Frank Sinatra and cup sizing for bras. We were before Batman, Grapes of Wrath, Rudolph the Red nosed Reindeer and Snoopy. Before DDT and vitamin pills, Vodka (in the United States)

and the white wine craze, disposable diapers, Jeeps and the Jefferson nickel. Before Scotch Tape, Grand Coulee Dam, M&M's, the automatic shift and the Lincoln Continental. When we were in college, pizzas, Cheerios, frozen orange juice, instant coffee and McDonalds were unheard of. We thought fast food was what you ate during Lent. We were before FM radio, tape recorders, electric typewriters, word processors, Muzak, electronic music, Rock 'n Roll, Rap and Disco dancing. Almost no one flew across the country and Trans-Atlantic flight belonged to Lindberg and Amelia Earhart. We were before Israel and the United Nations, before India, Pakistan, Indonesia, Iceland and the Philippines were independent countries. Since my graduation, 92 countries, 48 of them African, have become independent nations. We were before pantyhose, drip-dry clothes, icemakers, dishwashers, clothes dryers, freezers and electric blankets. Before Hawaii and Alaska became states. Before men wore long hair and women wore tuxedos.

We were before Leonard Bernstein, yogurt, Ann Landers, plastics, hair dryers, the 40-hour workweek and the minimum wage. We were before the Sexual Revolution, before the Pill and before the population explosion, which inexplicably, went hand in hand. We got married first, and then lived together. How really quaint can we be? We were before the "If it feels good, do it" philosophy. We were before AIDS. We were before condoms, in school and sex education classes on how to use them but who would have taught the classes anyhow?

In our day, cigarette smoking was fashionable, grass was mowed, Coke was something you drank and pot was something you cooked in. We were before coin vending machines, jet planes, helicopters and interstate highways. In 1937, American schools were not desegregated and blacks were not allowed to play in the Major Leagues and, oh yes, we were before Madeline O'Hare and before she got prayer out of the schools. In 1937, "Made In Japan" meant junk and the term "making out" referred to how you did on an exam. In our time there were 5 & 10-cent stores where you could buy things for 5 and 10 cents. For just a nickel, you could ride the subway or ride the ferry or make a phone call or buy a Coke, or buy enough stamps to mail one letter and two postcards. You could buy a new Chevy Coupe for just $659.00 but who could afford that in 1937? Not many, and that's a pity because gas was only ten cents a gallon. If anyone in those days had asked us to explain CIA, UFO, NATO, NFL, JFK, ERA, NASA, AIDS or IUD we would have said, "Alphabet soup"! We were not before the difference between the sexes was discovered, but we were before Christine Jorgenson and sex changes. We just made do with what we had and so it was in 1937! I am sure you could add many, many more to this list.

Whoever made up that list did a lot of research and I am sure you could add many more now, since that list was published. The old mind doesn't allow us to remember all that much and it's hard to imagine all those things came along after 1937 without seeing it in print to remind us. Here it is 2004 - what will the next 50 years bring?

I have witnessed a lot of bad in my time but I have witnessed so much good in the world as well. The advent of TV, although I don't know whether that should be classified as good but what would we do without it? We might have time to read some outstanding books. The advent of the computer is an amazing invention I have witnessed. Some of you may remember the old box camera. You are really dating yourself but I mention it only because of the fascinating developments in the camera industry. How it can be tied into your computer and the unbelievable things you can now do with the camera! It too is mind-boggling and way beyond my understanding.

How about the telephone of today? I remember when I was just a mite on the farm. Our telephone was in a bulky wooden box hanging on the wall. To make a call you cranked the handle two or three times and an operator came on with a "Yes, may I help you?" Once you gave her the name of the person you wanted connected to, you could hear two or three get in on the line to listen to your conversation. It was difficult to keep any secrets down on the farm in those days. Now, nearly every car has a telephone and it is unbelievable the number of calls received and made that people find necessary while driving. Who would ever have believed that someday you would be able to make a call on an instrument half the size of the palm of your hand and see the person with whom you are talking? That's one miracle that wasn't mentioned in the Bible!

Without the help of computers, who could imagine just a few years ago the developments made in space through the engineering magic of the NASA people? While living in Galesburg, my neighbor was a hard-nosed Cub fan. We had numerous discussions about the Cubs and I told him one time that we would have a man on the moon before the Cubs would win a World Series or even get into one! In my mind, I never believed for a minute that we would ever put a man on the moon, but we sure did. Have the Cubs ever gotten into a Series? Even as I write this book we have a space vehicle now circling Jupiter. It took seven years to travel the 2.2 billion miles to reach Jupiter so what do I know about space travel? I know just enough about space travel to know that I could never have been a part of it under any conditions not even when I was young and foolish! When we were living in Florida, on January 28, 1986, we were on a drive listening to the radio to two announcers describing the lift-off of the Space Shuttle Challenger. We were watching it through the windshield of the car when we heard "oh my goodness" and then complete silence. They then announced that the Challenger had blown up. As we watched we knew what had happened even before they had told the world.

On February 1st, 2003 we were watching the return of the Shuttle Columbia. Again, as we watched it was evident that the spaceship was disintegrating as Commander Rick Husband was preparing for re-entry into the Earth's atmosphere. To date, there hasn't been a shuttle up in space since. As complex as space flight is and probably will always be, even with the unbelievable progress that has been made in the program, we still have a lot to learn.

We have put three or four (and maybe more) un-manned vehicles on Mars to send pictures back of the terrain. I think there has been a lot of thought about putting a man on Mars someday and again I say, "Never!" I've been wrong before. Should it really happen before I die, I have a list of United States Senators that I could suggest for the initial trip. I won't mention any names because I'd bet that many of you have your own list and when combined with mine might include the entire Senate! I do agree with the addition of female astronauts because man has never been too good about asking for directions. All kidding aside, my hat is off to all the astronauts and the entire NASA organization. It boggles my earthbound mind when I try to imagine even the Jupiter vehicle sending back colored pictures from 2.2 billion miles in space!

With all of the successful exploration of space made by NASA it's rather easy to overlook the success made in the Aviation industry during and since World War II. When the Japanese hit Pearl Harbor on December 7th, 1941 the United States Air Force consisted mainly of the P-40 Fighter and the B-17 Heavy Bomber. Soon the B-25 Medium Bomber and the B-24 Heavy Bomber were put in circulation.

When the United States entered World War II, keep in mind that Germany had prepared years ahead for the war. They had millions of men in uniform; countless airplanes, tanks, submarines, Navy ships and trained leaders. One would have to believe that at that point they were far better prepared for war than we were. In 1941, the Japanese attacked; President Roosevelt declared war and miracles began to happen. In addition to the P-40 and B-17 planes we did have some tanks and our Navy was in pretty good shape and no doubt our Air Force was in better shape than I remember or knew. I was never up on the Naval Air Force or what kind of planes they had or in what kind of shape they were in. History will show that they did their job as well as the Army Air Force!

When I mentioned miracles I meant, first of all, and I can't express this enough, our nation came together behind President Roosevelt in all phases of the war effort. Everybody willingly got involved! There may have been protesters but I really can't recall any. Maybe it's because I don't want to remember them and what they represented.

A handful of ultra sharp and dedicated engineers put their heads together and designed the tools-of-war. This includes a number of fighter aircraft and medium bombers. They updated the B-17 and brought on the B-24 to assist the B-17. Not only were they designed but the manufacturing plants tooled up and the ordinary people joined the work force and produced (in record time) all of the necessary equipment. This, along with the many men and women who put on our nation's uniforms simply overwhelmed the Germans on the sea, air, and land. Let us not forget the many citizens who were out selling War Bonds to pay for the war.

In that four-year period between the Pearl Harbor hit in 1941 and the end of the war in 1945 the engineers and the civilian labor force designed and delivered aircraft that included the P-38, P-39, P-47, P-51, P-61 and P-63 (these in addition to the P-40 and B-17 already in service). These were all propeller driven fighters designed to combat enemy fighters. This included the P-47 and P-51 that rode shotgun for the 17's and 24's to their targets over Germany and beyond. The P-61 was primarily a night fighter, although it may have been used for other duty. They brought forth the B-25 and the B-26 medium bombers and the A-20, A-24 and the A-26 low level attack planes as well as bombers. The C-46 and C-47 were manufactured using the DC-3 commercial airliner platform. Then the B-29 came out midway through the war and was used in the Pacific Theater only. It performed superbly and is best remembered as the "super fort" Enola Gay that dropped the first operational atomic bomb on Hiroshima. Three days later a second bomb was to be dropped from another B-29 named Bock's Car flown by Charles Sweeney. The primary target was to be Kokura, Japan but it was covered with clouds and smoke, and after several passes over that target it was finally abandoned. Nagasaki was chosen instead. The result was the death of 70,000 people. On August 14th the Japanese surrendered. On September 2nd a formal surrender ceremony occurred aboard the battleship Missouri with an armada of 1,900 planes including 462 B-29's performing a dramatic fly over. Only recently did the pilot of the Enola Gay, Colonel Paul Tibbets Jr., die. Coincidently, General Charles Sweeney died within the same week at the age of 84. That Atomic bomb was the first one he dropped and he was only 25 years old at the time.

No airplane in the Air Corps had the versatility that the C-47 enjoyed. In addition to adapting to every kind of cargo imaginable I have discovered the C-47's were converted into gun-ships in Vietnam. These C-47's had three multi-barrelled 7.62mm Gatling guns mounted on the left side of the plane, two mounted out of converted windows and the third mounted on the floor sticking out of half of a double door. For treetop flying I imagine it functioned as a gunship very well.

With the advent of the jet engine, it is truly amazing what four engines in a plane can lift off the ground, compared to the C-47. For our use with the paddle propellers the maximum take off weight was 29,300 pounds. Maximum range was roughly 1500 miles with a top speed of 232 mph. Today there is the C-5A Galaxy and the C-17 Globemaster. The C-5A is a four-engine plane with a maximum take-off weight of 837,000 pounds, a maximum range of 3,749 miles and a top speed of 571 mph. It has a fuel capacity of 51,154 gallons. How would you like to fill that dude at $2.00 a gallon?

I never got the gross take off weight on the C-17 Globemaster but it did give this load variety: 102 paratroopers or 3 apache helicopter gun ships plus fifty troops, or one mobile Howitzer and its ammunition vehicle, two Humvees and a 2.5 ton truck with 32 troops. As I've said many times, every vehicle is designed to do a certain job and then there is the C-47 to do whatever is left. The C-47 did whatever it was called upon to do and then land on a dollar bill and give you 50 cents change! In addition to its operational versatility, its other greatest asset was its ability to land and take off in very short, sometimes ungodly, fields. In its original design as a commercial airliner I doubt that the engineers had a clue on what it would be called upon to do in wartime.

The jet was just coming off the drawing boards at the end of the war. The Germans had gotten the twin engine Messerschmitt ME262A into combat at the very end of the war. My research stated that Germany had managed to deliver 1,320 planes in thirteen months and nearly 300 a month by the end of the war. Had Germany had the Messerschmitt ME262A earlier in the war, they might have been more difficult to defeat. Our gutsy pilots in the P-47's and P-51's must have figured out a way to beat the Messerschmitts because I have never read where there was too much trouble.

The United States had also designed a jet by the end of the war but never got it into combat in Europe. It was the P-80 - a truly beautiful airplane. My buddy, Archey and I were in Rome once and were fortunate enough to be on the airfield when a Colonel from the States was there to give General Eaker a demonstration of a P-80. It was obviously the first airplane I had seen without propellers and not knowing a thing about the jet engine I thought, "How in the hell did he get it here and how in the hell is he going to get it off the ground?" It was truly an amazing demonstration, akin to witnessing the invention of the wheel. I really don't know how much combat, if any, the P-80 got. We have such fantastic jets now and that P-80 wouldn't have a chance. Interestingly enough the P-80's were made into the T-33 trainers that astronauts use.

Now that you have grasped the size of the C-47 and partially grasped the size of the C-5A and the C-17 let me blow your mind with the Russian made Cossack. The Cossack is the world's largest plane. It has a wingspan of 290 feet, six jet

147

engines each developing 51,590 pounds of thrust requiring a runway at least 11,400 feet long. Its maximum take off weight is (grab a chair) 1,322,770 pounds. If and when it does get off the ground its cruising speed is 530 miles per hour. Maximum range without refueling is 2,795 miles. If it had trouble I doubt it could find an emergency field even in the flattest parts of Texas. It was built in Kiev, Ukraine and made its maiden flight on December 21st, 1988. The article never said if it ever landed. It has 28 wheels of which 20 can be steered and can carry a 551,000-pound payload. I would like to see the crew try to land that baby in a valley field of Yugoslavia at night like the C-47 with no landing accidents. Again, every vehicle has a designed purpose. I've been trying to figure out what the purpose was for this behemoth. Perhaps it was to evacuate the entire city of Moscow if needed.

I would like to get back to my trip to the WWII Memorial. It was one of the highlights of my many years on this earth. Ron drove his van and I just rode along. We left on May 26th and went as far as Washington, Pennsylvania and then on to Washington D.C. on the 27th. We met with Ron's friend Byron Crozier, his wife Beth and his son John all who had arrived earlier. Byron, a Marine and Navy man in WWII was kind enough to provide the Foreword for this book. He was the one who put this trip together and even arranged for us to stay in Washington with a friend of John's. John is a veteran of Vietnam. Byron's grandsons lived and worked in Washington and knew the city like the back of their hands. Anytime, anywhere we needed to go, they delivered us. When we were done they would pick us up. I can only imagine the amount of walking they saved us.

The Friday before the formal ceremony, we went to the Memorial. We saw it in its entirety. For lack of a more descriptive word I can only say that I was overwhelmed and will attempt to paint a picture of what we witnessed. A very large crowd was moving slowly around with many veterans in wheelchairs. My first thought at seeing the Memorial was, "how did they get this incredible location?" One view was the Washington Monument with the Lincoln Memorial at 180 degrees the other way. It's as if this space had been waiting for this very Memorial. Even though it was hot, the day was beautiful. I suspect that Byron had some political pull with Senator Lugar's office because we had excellent reserved seats.

Let me share some of the tributes from the Saturday Dedication Ceremony.

The excerpts below are from the program, *The Dedication of the National World War II Memorial, Washington D.C. May 29, 2004.*

Here in the presence of Washington and Lincoln, one, the eighteenth century father and the other the nineteenth century preserver of our nation, we honor those twentieth century Americans who took up the struggle during the Second World War and made the sacrifices to perpetuate the gift our forefathers entrusted to us: a nation conceived in liberty and justice.

Richard D. Harvey

From George W. Bush: Greetings to those gathered to celebrate the dedication of the National World War II Memorial on the National Mall.

Our nation is strong because of the brave men and women who have sacrificed to protect the Democratic ideals that are the foundation of America. After the Second World War returning veterans often said they had just done their jobs. Yet, these proud citizens and their family members knew the stakes of the fight they had been in and the magnitude of what they had achieved. They had maintained the greatest fighting force in the world, defeated tyranny in Europe and Asia, and kept our country free.

This memorial honors the sixteen million Americans who served in the United States Armed Forces during World War II, the more than four hundred thousand who died and the millions who supported the war effort from home. As a new part of our National landscape, it stands as a lasting tribute to the contributions of those heroes who preserved liberty's blessings.

Today as we fight a war against terror we remember our veterans' commitment to our country and their legacy of patriotism. By answering the call of duty and risking their lives to protect their fellow citizens, these patriots continue to inspire all Americans.

Laura joins me in sending our best wishes. May God bless you and may God continue to bless the United States of America.

From General P.X. Kelley, General United States Marine Corps (Ret.), Chairman: In 1993 the American Battle Monuments Commission, an independent agency of the executive branch of the Federal Government, was authorized by the 103rd congress to establish a memorial to honor those who served their country during World War II, and to commemorate our participation in a war that lasted for almost four years.

Our Commission acknowledges and praises the many and significant contributions of our predecessors. Under the leadership of General Fred Woerner, U.S. Army (Ret.), former Chairman of the Commission and Mr. Pete Wheeler, Chairman of the Memorial Advisory Board, they nurtured the memorial through many of its formative years. We also are thankful to the many people who joined together in creating this magnificent testimonial. This includes support from the administration, the Congress, the design team and our many contractors.

Needless to say, none of this would have been possible without the dedicated leadership of former Senator Bob Dole, Chairman of the memorial fund-raising Campaign and FedEx Chairman Fred Smith, the campaign Co-chairman, or Tom Hanks, who also volunteered his time to be our national spokesman. Finally, I especially want to send my heartfelt gratitude to those whose contributions made this Memorial a reality.

To those we honor here today, let me simply say, "God bless America, the land of the free, but only so long as it is the home of the brave."

From Bob Dole, National Chairman World War II Memorial Campaign and Frederick W. Smith, National Co-Chairman World War II Memorial Campaign: After many years of planning, fund-raising and construction, the World War II Memorial is finally completed. It stands on this historic site as a lasting tribute to the brave men and women who served so valiantly during that era. While the architecture and artistry are at last achieved, the memorial is only just realizing its greatness.

The presence of all of you here today, at this dedication to your honor, bravery, and memory, is what will be the defining element of its grace and stature in years to come. The people who so selflessly joined together to defeat tyranny through heroic deeds and countless sacrifices, coming together again to dedicate a permanent memorial to their achievements and those of so many who fought, lived and worked with them.

Many of the heroes of that great conflict came home and built a nation that remains the world's most powerful example of democracy and freedom in action. Many others did not return, did not live to see the fruits of their sacrifice. Many more have been lost in the years since, but their memories are with us and will instill these granite walls with the courage and fortitude to inspire future generations to greatness when their nation calls. Thank you for being a part of this memorable day.

This entry has no author but describes the Memorial very well. It is titled, *National World War II Memorial, a tribute to a generation.*

The Second World War was the largest and most devastating war in history. Freedom was threatened as never before. In a show of resolve and unity this country had never before experienced, Americans from all walks of life joined together to defeat tyranny. Sixteen million served in uniform. Millions worked at home building the world's Arsenal of Democracy. More than 400,000 Americans gave their lives. The National World War II Memorial creates a special place to commemorate the sacrifice and celebrate the victory of World War II, the only 20th Century event commemorated on the Mall's central axis. Built into the granite and bronze of the Memorial are symbols of special significance. Two flagpoles frame the ceremonial entrance with the service seals of the Army, Navy, Marine Corps, Army Air Forces, Coast Guard and Merchant Marine. Along the ceremonial ramp that leads into the plaza are 24 base-relief panels that depict Americans at war, at home as well as overseas. Inscriptions reflect a generation's spirit, commitment, and willingness to sacrifice for a cause greater than them.

Two pavilions serve as markers and entries on the north and south ends of the plaza. Within the pavilions, four American eagles hold a suspended laurel wreath to memorialize the victory of the World War II generation. Inlayed on the floors is the World War II Victory Medal surrounded by the years 1941-1945 and the words, Victory on land, Victory in the air.

Fifty-six pillars, bound by sculptured ropes, celebrate the unprecedented unity of the nation. Each state and territory from that period and the District of Columbia are represented by a pillar adorned with oak and wheat wreaths, the symbols of the industrial and agricultural might of the nation, and inscribed with its name. Within a commemorative area at the western side of the Memorial a field of 4,000 sculpted gold stars on the freedom wall honors the more than 400,000 Americans who gave their lives. During the war the gold star was the symbol of a family member who had died.

The historic waterworks of the rainbow pool have been restored and contribute to the celebratory nature of the Memorial. Semi-circular fountains at the base of the two pavilions and waterfalls flanking the freedom wall complement the waterworks in the rainbow pool.

The design elements create a sense of place that is distinct, memorable, evocative and serene. The Memorial now stands, as a powerful symbol of the national will to sacrifice for the Democratic ideals that shaped our foundation and direct our future.

President Harry S. Truman wrote: Our debt to the heroic men and valiant women in the service of our country can never be repaid. They have earned our undying gratitude. America will never forget their sacrifices.

I had read about the Memorial and the work that Bob Dole had put into it, but I never thought that I would get the chance to see it. Now I have seen it and my thanks to Byron

Crozier for putting the trip together and to my son, Ron, for taking me. As a proud WWII veteran, the visit was an unforgettable experience and the Memorial is a great tribute to all veterans of the Second World War. I was trained to do a small part in that war and was fortunate to have made it home. All through the years I have never forgotten my friends in the service who all felt proud about our place in history. Our generation fought a battle for freedom and democracy and many gave their lives. Those 400,000, who fell, never to enjoy the freedom and prosperity for which they gave the ultimate sacrifice, are truly the ones this Memorial honors. President Truman said, "America will never forget their sacrifices" and this Memorial assures that.

Many books have been written about the heroes from the various services, each one more than deserving of the honor that was paid them. However, for every hero officially honored, there are hundreds more who, for whatever reason, never had an opportunity to relate his or her heroic story. There are super heroes like the ones written about but I believe that every person whether he or she was drafted or enlisted and who served on foreign soil, is a hero. Let's not forget those in uniform who served stateside and who turned out the Weapons of War, for they were just as important. Without their dedicated input on this side we would have been in a heap-of-trouble on the other side! I believe there were many unheralded heroes along with many super heroes – some still living as well as the over 400,000 people who gave their lives.

As I struggle to put the finishing touch to this book, dwelling on and having lived through World War II, and having been an interested bystander during the Korean War, the Vietnam War, the Gulf War and now the "Forever War" against the worldwide terrorists, constantly on my mind are the protestors. I can't help but wonder if through this century had the protestors been making the governmental decisions, what language would we be speaking here in America - maybe German or Korean or Japanese or Vietnamese or maybe Arabic? With the worldwide threat of terrorism, I doubt that we, as Americans, will again enjoy the freedom we enjoyed prior to September 11th, 2001 until every last terrorist is defeated. I don't believe we can exist in the present world by turning the other cheek. I believe speak softly (or better yet, loudly) and carry a big stick is a better philosophy. Thank the good Lord that President Bush had the foresight to recognize the danger and had the courage and fortitude to do something about it. America must be the victor, regardless of the cost!

Through the turbulent centuries, we certainly have learned that FREEDOM is not free but that FREEDOM is super costly. When FREEDOM has been gained by our courageous forefathers we need to give thanks to any and all Veterans, pray for a protestor (for they know not what they are doing!), cherish this FREEDOM that we too often take for granted and, live and enjoy life to the fullest everyday! Allow me to close this chapter and book with these words by President Ronald Regan in his farewell address to the nation on January 11th, 1989, he warned, "America had to better convey that America is freedom: FREEDOM of Speech - - FREEDOM of Religion

- - FREEDOM of Enterprise - - and freedom is precious and rare. It's fragile and it needs protection".

If a reader, especially anyone from the 60th Troop Carrier Group would like to get in touch with the author, please contact the publisher for information. AuthorHouse, #888-728-8467 or www.authorhouse.com.

ABOUT THE AUTHOR

I have heard that most war vets don't volunteer conversation of time-spent serving. They claim 'it was their duty – something that had to be done'. The author of this book, Lt. Richard Harvey, my grandfather, is no different than I suspect any WWII veteran. His response to any inquiry about his time at war always was "Now why would you want to know about that?" I also imagine that if briefly engaged, any vets stories, experiences and memories would begin to flow like lava from Mt. Vesuvius.

My grandfather and I don't share similar political views – especially about our country's obligation to fight, and our religious views vary widely. I can only assume that my passion for the written word comes from a bloodline that bonds us without prejudice. I, like he, have an appreciation for the untold story. It is said that the current war in Iraq may be the first of many that will not have an historical paper trail due in part to the omnipresent use of the Internet. School textbooks will no doubt continue to adequately provide an historical view of any world event for prosperity's sake. However, will there be room for the slice of life accounts of a 22-year old soldier who is out of his element trying to make the most of a curious situation? With more than 1,200 WWII vets passing away daily, personal accounts, written or recorded by family may be the only memoirs we have to reflect upon.

There are no particular heroics displayed within the pages of *The C-47 – Flying Workhorse of WWII* only a series of moments marked by emotion, compassion, patriotism and loyalty to an oath taken before God and country. If one takes the time to engage anyone who has experienced an event such as war, we may continue a quilt of memories from which future generations can enjoy, gather inspiration and experience a fleeting moment of the past.

CPSIA information can be obtained at www.ICGtesting.com
Printed in the USA
LVOW132350270513

335590LV00004BA/861/A